Mel Bay Presents

Key to Five-String BANJO

HOME IMPROVISATION WORKSHOP

By Pat Cloud

In Memory of Don Reno

My appreciation and thanks to: Patrick Brayer, Nancy Cloud, Dana Thorin, Robert Leach UCSD, David Crisler, Douglas Dillard, Bill Keith, Tony Trischka, Donald Lanning, John Lawless and John Delgatto of Sierra Records.

Special thanks to Jack Hatfield for final editing.

CD CONTENTS

1 Welcome!/Tuning [1:29]	14 Exercise 8 [:24]	27 Position 2 [:18]	40 Melodic Fingering [1:03]
2 Position 1 [:21]	15 Exercise 9 [:30]	28 Position 3 [:18]	41 Embellished Version [1:04]
3 Position 2 [:20]	16 Exercise 10 [:32]	29 Position 4 [:16]	42 D7 Ex. / G7 Ex. / C7 Ex. [:40]
4 Position 3 [:16]	17 Exercise 11 [:29]	30 Position 5 [:23]	43 Full Range Fingerings G7 [:20]
5 Position 4 [:18]	18 Exercise 12 [:23]	31 Open Fingerings / Exercise 1 [:18]	44 Full Range Fingerings C7 [:18]
6 Position 5 [:23]	19 Exercise 13 [:33]	32 Exercise 2 [:19]	45 Full Range Fingerings D7 [:16]
7 Exercise 1 [:37]	20 Exercise 14 [:34]	33 Exercise 3 [:19]	46 One Fret Blues / Exercise 1 [:29]
8 Exercise 2 [:20]	21 Position 1 [:35]	34 Exercise 4 [:17]	47 Exercise 2 [:26]
9 Exercise 3 [:24]	22 Position 2 [:36]	35 Exercise 5 [:17]	48 Exercise 3 [:28]
10 Exercise 4 [:28]	23 Position 3 [:33]	36 Full Range Arpeggios G/Em [:26]	49 Exercise 4 [:40]
11 Exercise 5 [:24]	24 Position 4 [:34]	37 C/Am [:25]	
12 Exercise 6 [:26]	25 Position 5 [:32]	38 D/Bm [:26]	
13 Exercise 7 [:23]	26 Exercises G-C-D Pos. 1 [:24]	39 Sally Johnson [1:06]	

© 1999 BY MEL BAY PUBLICATIONS, INC., PACIFIC, MO 63069.
ALL RIGHTS RESERVED. INTERNATIONAL COPYRIGHT SECURED. B.M.I. MADE AND PRINTED IN U.S.A.
No part of this publication may be reproduced in whole or in part, or stored in a retrieval system, or transmitted in any form or by any means, electronic, mechanical, photocopy, recording, or otherwise, without written permission of the publisher.

Visit us on the Web at http://www.melbay.com — E-mail us at email@melbay.com

INTRODUCTION

In my early teens, I heard my first Earl Scruggs album. Here was someone who had created his own musical world and lived in it. It was as if he was telling the whole world through his music, "Look here what I found!" He revealed through his music a world of rare musical joy he had found for himself with that old Mastertone. My immediate impulse after listening to the legendary "Foggy Mountain Banjo" album was "I want to do that too."

Because the banjo is a relatively new instrument from a folk heritage, it is stylistically tied to the musical personalities who contributed to its popularity. These great banjo personalities became synonymous with the techniques they used like "Seeger" or "Scruggs" or "Reno" style. These legendary artists had also found their way to that place that sparkled with sound.

The question most asked at workshops is, "How does one gain greater freedom of expression outside of basic chords and songs? How do you make up licks and phrases?"

Most students start by learning songs. While this is very desirable initially, the same old songs, once they have been technically mastered, pose a dilemma. They tend to limit the student to certain areas of the neck, thus fostering a polarized perception of the fretboard. The complaint of too little progress is often heard.

It is from this need for basic information that this instruction series begins. Most students aren't looking for intense theoretical knowledge, but rather something a little more "hands-on" to break the "I only know five songs" syndrome. The premise of this first book proposes that you visualize and see some of the tunes you already know in a new perspective. Its purpose is to shed light on simple connections unique to five string-banjo. This includes closed position fingerings as well as the open-string fingerings which can be found throughout the entire range of the neck.

The process of learning a musical instrument has an unconscious element that really can't be taught. You must go beyond the forms to *sound consciousness.* All players share a good deal of fretboard positions in common, although they do not always have a shared perception of those positions. This is why it is interesting to watch the left hand of great players. It tells much of how they depart from chord forms and "think" sounds into existence. While there is an agreed upon structure of major and minor chord forms from which players extract their licks, phrases and musical ideas, there is also an indefinable quality which can only be described as a kind of artistic eccentricity.

This sound consciousness can be initially realized by finding an underlying strata or "fingerprint" of the banjo neck. By visualizing and using this "road map," one identifies familiar patterns (songs, licks, etc.) within a structure and can then utilize them unconsciously to a musical end.

Basic chord forms provide a start for most beginning students, but what lies between those forms is a mystery. Geometric shapes linked to those forms provide a guide, however, what is needed is an all-encompassing template.

This is a book of sound perception. Although tab is initially used to find notes, you will make greater progress if you rely on tab as a last resort. The ideas in this book will help you break the habit of thinking in limited areas of the neck. Included are exercises which will expand your physical and conceptual abilities. You will utilize both the "along the string" or single string technique "across string" or arpa style (sometimes referred to as "melodic"). The total scope of style and invention possibilities for this unique instrument must include both.

With the integration of the 5th string, the singular character of the five string banjo neck appears. A musician who wishes to be complete or simply better informed will want to utilize as many techniques as possible, including the fifth string and the open/across string approach to shift to different registers on the fretboard. While this volume does not technically go into all keys, forthcoming books will do so and also address such topics as tonal centers, modulation and composition.

The emphasis in this volume will be on an overall sound-grid which is divided into five basic positions representing two basic sounds. When practiced in specific exercises, the component positions in this grid can be easily linked to reveal a greater perspective.

There isn't anything about "good" or "bad" playing habits, nor will there be anything about how anyone else "does it." There are many books on the market with great songs, licks and phrases. This book will help in showing how and why all these things fit together. It will also show you how you can always know exactly where you are on the fretboard.

It is assumed that you have access to a good instructor. It is also assumed that you have a basic grasp of three-finger technique. It is advised that you review the three basic major and minor chord forms before proceeding. There is nothing really mysterious about how the five-string banjo works. The banjo neck is designed a certain way. The exercises herein were invented to change how you think about the neck - the inward perception. If practiced patiently and persistently, they will yield a new sound consciousness from which a more creative direction can emerge. It is my hope that what is in your ears and your mind can at last enter your hands.

Play On!

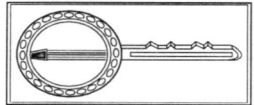 **The Key To Five String Banjo**

Foreword

The Five Colors Blind the Eye,
The Five Tones Deafen the Ear
The Five Flavors Dull the Taste

                                                        Lao Tzu, 565 B.C.

Everybody is looking for the magic bullet. Whether it be a crankcase additive remedy for an old jalopy that burns too much oil, or a Unified Field Theory conceived by a genius in physics, that search for a panacea to the illusive problem at hand is proverbial.

And so it goes with music. After thirty years a student and teacher of 5 string banjo, it is my observation that the average banjoist usually has a banjo case full of tab they can't play. Many books have been written about the art of five-string banjo, but all too few of them shed any light on a basic understanding of the fretboard beyond tabbed songs. Instead of fostering inventive possibilities, the fretboard poses a rather confusing and limiting enigma. And while nothing takes the place of practice and hard work, very few methods teach how to practice for the greatest results. And just what defines "results?"

Just what goals do you have? Is it the learning of five, ten or twenty songs and being able to play them in a band? Is it learning to compose your own arrangements or learning "backup" improvisation? Is it just playing what comes to mind? Any one of these goals is valid, for each leads naturally to the other.

Instead of a mythical bullet, there is practice and a plan. The best plans are simple and produce the greatest mileage for the effort put forth. The basis for the best musical plan is to remove any intermediary impediments (such as reliance on tablature, forms, etc.), thereby entering directly into the world of sound. Such a goal is easy to state but harder to accomplish.

In a world of sound, the hands do what the ears hear. In a world of sound, you are the listener as well as the player. In a world of sound, something beyond your conscious personality takes over and you do more than you ever thought you could. The possibilities on the fretboard become boundless. This is what I want for you, dear reader. It is an experience you won't want to miss. It can happen for you if you want it badly enough.

Patrick Cloud
Bishop, CA., 1997

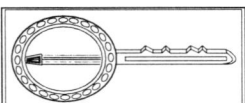

The Key To Five String Banjo

Contents

What! Not Another Banjo Book! 6
The Key Banjo Icons 7
The Key To Five String Banjo! 8
Practice Tips 9
Total View 13
About Right and Left Hand Technique 14
Into Action! 17
Now Hear This 21
Exercises On G/Em 22
Open String Exercises 24
Interval Studies 27
Position Shifts 28
G-C-D in the first position 30
Exercises For G-C-D 31
G/Em 33
C/Am 33
D/Bm 33
Song Study: Sally Johnson 34
Dominant Seventh Chord 37
G major scale: 37
D7 chord 37
Changing One Note - Again! 40
Practical Theory Appendix 46
Major Chord Triads 47
The Pentatonic Scale 48
The Dominant Progression 49
Where Are The Notes On This Thing? 50
Jazzin' It Up Appendix 51
What is Improvisation? 52
Extended Harmony 53
G Seventh Scale: 53
Riding the Cycle 54-55
About the Author 56

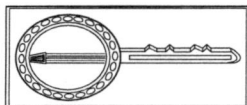

The Key To Five String Banjo

What! Not Another Banjo Book!

Taking the "Fret" Out of Your Fretboard

Oh no! Another banjo instruction book! You might be thinking, "I have eleven already. They're over there propping open the screen door so the dog can get in and out without me having to get up from the couch. I get half way through them before I lose interest and they end up in the screen door pile."

Books are great. They have essential information and loads of tab. (They may even have centerfolds of your favorite banjo.) But often, they lack one important thing. If I may use the tired road map analogy:

You have this map (banjo instruction book). On the map are highways, roads, trails, mountains lakes, rivers, streams towns and cities (tabbed songs, chords, picking patterns, licks, etc.). You know the main highways and sort of know some of the roads. You know how to get in and out of the towns well enough (tabbed songs). If you do stray, you can always refer back to the map (tab) or stop at a gas station, and how to get to a place not on the map (ask a teacher). Asking for directions may be of no use unless you find someone who is a native or a Highway Patrol officer, because people are familiar only with their own area. There are landmarks and places that only the locals know about (sometimes you can find what you want in a book or from a teacher, sometimes not).

What if you came across a banjo map that can reveal to you key landmarks which will get you around the neck more quickly and with less hassle? Such a map would tell you about things you already know and also provide additional information that will increase creative possibilities. In other words, it would build on what you already know and make it easier for you to navigate to sounds you don't know or may have never known existed. Hopefully, this book is that map.

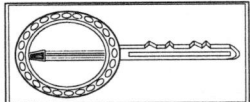 **The Key To Five String Banjo**

The Key Banjo Icons

The following markers are to alert you to key ideas or action related steps. They are used to guide you toward those things in the text you are most interested in and will let you know what to skip when you are not. A large audience is addressed by instruction books. Not everyone is interested in the more theoretical aspects of music. For those who are interested, an icon will point to a supplementary appendix for greater understanding. For those that are not, they can skip the theory and get to playing!

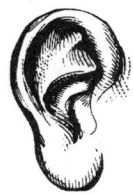 **Ear** - This indicates required listening on the included recording. Listen first before playing the tab.

 **Hand & Key** - This will refer you to an appendix at the end of the book for a better in-depth explanation, usually involving practical theory.

 **Jazz Band** - This is useful for people interested in improvisation in a jazz context.

 **Exercise** - This indicates exercise(s) which will work your hands for greater facility.

 **Rabbit** - "If it's a rabbit, you'd better grab it!" This is an essential key idea which, when played and listened to, will deepen your understanding and sound perception. Have your banjo in your hands to play it!

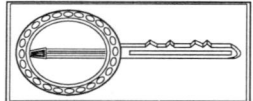

The Key To Five String Banjo

Now listen up! Here it is!

The Key To Five String Banjo!

(see below)

Practice. Playing a lot. You knew it all along, right? The very word may bring childhood visions of a stern piano teacher with a wooden ruler ready to rap your knuckles for hitting a "clam." To some, practice feels like punishment. What should be an exploratory adventure in creativity is instead prison-style drudgery at the rockpile. Well, maybe not that bad, but close! Yes, I know of all the resolves. You get a new book and promise yourself to practice religiously. You even plan to give up Thursday night bowling! But alas! Something always comes up to break the habit of sitting down at the same time every day and devoting to that beautiful expensive instrument the time you promised it. To compound the problem, you get even more discouraged when you listen to your favorite tape or CD. You think, "I'll never get to that point." Take heart! You can get into a practice routine which will move you forward toward your goal! You may even (heaven forbid!) look forward to your practice session!

Keep in mind that practicing is not the only consideration. It is practicing with a method and a purpose that moves you toward your goal. The goal is important. Practicing on a song is different from the practice you will receive in this book. The object of this book is to lay down a usable grid or pattern which codifies the neck and all its possibilities. This "road map" will help you become aware of where you are on the neck. It will also teach your ear about the chord quality suggested by the notes you select. Here are a few tips for practice motivation and consistency:

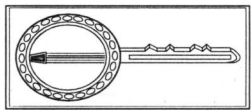

Practice Tips

Pick up the banjo once a day whether you play it or not.

1.) Instead of making yourself promises that you cannot keep, pick up the banjo once a day whether you play it or not. Take it out, hold it, play one or two right hand patterns. Then, if you have more pressing things to do or you really don't want to play at that time, put it away! The idea is to touch it EVERY DAY! You may touch it two or three times a day if you want! Remember that two 15 minute "touching" sessions add up to a half hour. If you don't have time for a regular practice session, then touch it five minutes for that day and put it back. Some people use an instrument stand so they won't have to keep taking their banjo in and out of the case. There is a psychology involved here. The fact that you are at least making an effort and not surrendering to complacency will help. The idea here is to take it one day at a time. Surely you can be committed for three to five minutes in a single day? This is plenty of time to accomplish a connection on a daily basis.

Get A Calendar

2.) Get a calendar, preferably one with places you can write in. This calendar is for recording your practice habits. On it you can write what you practiced or whether you managed to pick up your banjo. Keep this calendar near your practice area. When you touch your banjo three to five minutes, make an X for that day and note the time. When you sit down and play for more than 15 minutes, make a check mark or any doodle you want on the calendar. When you sit down for a half-hour or more make a star. Set yourself a goal of a minimum number of checks and stars for that month and write it on the top of the calendar. At the end of the month tally up your marks to see if you met your goal.

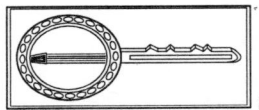

The Key To Five String Banjo

Practice Spot

3.) One of the most important aspects of consistent productive practicing is the environment in which you sit down with your banjo. It may not seem important at first, but think about it. If you have a location where the "magic" is likely to happen, it helps to create a frame of mind which fosters consistency and purpose. If you have the space at home, make it as isolated from distractions as possible. If that is not currently possible, then you must make do with a chair and a desk. If you have a tape recorder, music stand and metronome, great! Place your practice calendar where you can see it. You might also surround the area with pictures of your favorite banjo player in concert or photos of memorable times at festivals. Your banjo practice space might be a an area at work where you are alone while everybody else goes to lunch. Some people can make great progress during their half hour lunch break. The point is to make it your area and your time in which you can build your understanding and skill on a daily basis.

If you are a person who has a less flexible job routine precluding a lunchtime practice session, decide whether it would be most beneficial to practice before or after work. Working an hour's practice a day into your daily routine is the goal. If you are tired after work, it is hard to get motivated. If you have a chance to relax after a day's work, then a great time to practice is before or after dinner. Forget television - you don't really want to see all the bad news anyway. Replace it with some banjo time.

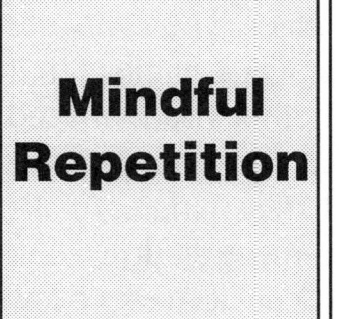

Mindful Repetition

4.) Every fingering problem bows to repetition. Slow down to a crawl and study whether your finger habits are correct for that phrase. Playing purposely slow to see where you are having problems makes for mindful practice. So does awareness of the chord changes as you gradually increase speed. If a portion of a song is giving you problems and is slowing you down, isolate it for study. Play through each of these trouble spots ten times, counting each one only if you play it correctly. If you still cannot bring it up to speed after inserting it back into the song, either consider whether to alter the fingering or consult your teacher for advice.

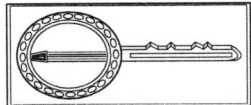

The Key To Five String Banjo

One Phrase At A Time

5.) Build your song or solo by starting with small portions and linking them together. The actual link or point at which you divided the exercise up for study requires proper attention in order to make the transition go smoothly. You are striving for awareness of the total picture. The sound you seek will naturally emerge as you increase speed. Never sacrifice timing or form for speed. Speed usually comes of its own accord as you gain familiarity. Try to convert the tab to sound and be guided by sound.

Know Where You Are

6.) Knowing where you are in relation to the song as a whole is essential. This means knowing the chord you are playing over and where it changes. Practicing an exercise or solo includes knowing what chord harmonizes the passage you are moving in and out of. If you are breaking up a piece for study by chord changes, keep the chord sound in mind as you practice the lick or fragment over it. When playing the piece as a whole, you should be able to feel where the chord changes occur.

Solve Fingering Problems

7.) Before increasing speed, solve fingering problems that are hindering you. Problems in fingering can result from hesitation that is caused by lack of physical advantage or they may involve leverage you have over the left and right hand activities. Strengthening the hands by slow repetition can help. Always have a finger ready for the next indicated move. Often, when you break up a song to learn it in fragments, the transition between the sections looses continuity. This may be where some fingering problems exist. A good instructor will tell you if your approach is going to yield results before you invest time in a certain fingering. If playing a song or exercise slowly doesn't give you that final satisfying effect, patience is required. Soon your efforts will start to pay off as you gain speed. Take your time and make absolutely sure that your fingering is accessible and fluid. As for the right hand, try to eliminate unneeded movement in picking.

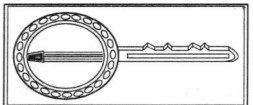

The Key To Five String Banjo

Set Sensible Goals

8.) It is a good idea to set reasonable, attainable goals for a certain time period. You have only NOW to practice. Specifically, this day and the moment you sit down at your practice area. Suppose you decide to make an hour a day your goal. You will make more progress by knowing how much time you spend on each exercise. Decide what you want to accomplish in that hour and note it on your calendar. If you bite off more than you can chew in an hour, then divide your original goal in half. A timer set to ten or fifteen minute sessions for each exercise can help you move through your practice hour more effectively. Eventually you will determine what is realistic for you. As you progress, you will be able to accomplish more in one hour than you previously did in five. Taking compulsive stabs at material that is too difficult will result in disillusionment and a sense of defeat. A competent instructor will help to avoid this. Always take a break every thirty minutes.

Use A Tape Recorder

9.) The use of a tape recorder is not only wise, it is mandatory! Much can be learned by recording yourself and playing it back. It is encouraging to record your practice sessions, to monitor your progress as the days go by. A tape recorder with a half speed control is preferable. When you are learning, you cannot play fast enough to realize the final effect you are striving for. Listening to a song played slowly gives you the feel of the finished product. Listening to half-speed recordings will help you move from over-dependence on tablature to dependence upon sound. You can never go wrong with sound. When you get down to it, that's all there really is.

Many tape recorders have a half-speed control. The most popular brand name that comes to mind is Marantz. There are also mini-cassette recorders that feature a slow speed button for recording lectures. These are also useful for slowing down music.

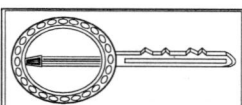

The Key To Five String Banjo

The Total View

Knowledge is indeed powerful. Just a little bit of it, applied properly, can go a long way. Learning songs by tabulature is a different kind of learning than learning the neck. Learning the neck is finding where all the sounds are and naming them. Let's follow the road map analogy further: Learning your first song by tabulature is like finding a road through an unfamiliar area on a map. You only see one sliver of the whole pie. You also may have learned that certain "clumps" of notes form chords. As you learn more songs and chords, you find out more and more about the wilderness called the fretboard. Actually, it's not a wilderness at all! What a person knows or visualizes about the banjo neck is a direct result of all the songs they have learned, from the first to the most recent. The problem is how to organize all these sound elements.

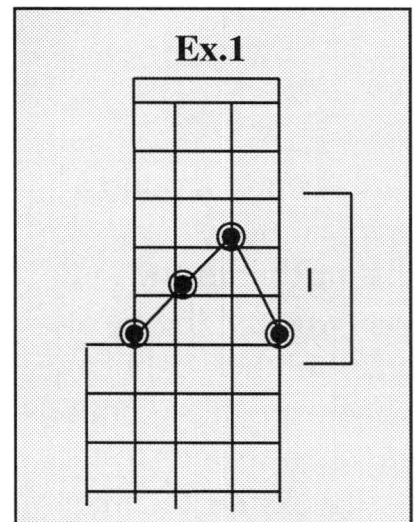

Something to Hang Your Hat On

A method or a system for the banjo neck must be simple and easily adapted to many different chord types. It must also be accessible to both single string and arpa style playing. Most music theory is not practical until you work it into the instrument and use it. Practical music theory is designed to be active in your visualization of the neck. It should give you the most "bang for the buck." Most good ideas are simple. The best way to impart a simple idea is to relate it to something which is already familiar. You must have a basic concept to "hang your hat on" so to speak. Because of its familiarity, a G major chord makes a great "hat rack" to begin with. **(Ex. 1)**

Ever wonder why certain notes make a G chord? Find out about the basic chord position shown above and its related positions in the Practical Theory Appendix, p. 47.

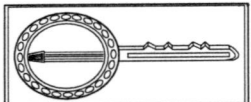

The Key To Five String Banjo

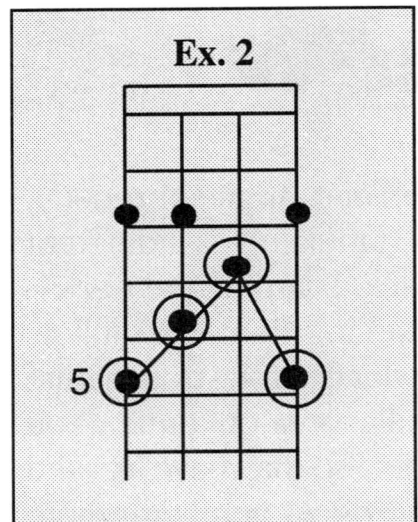

If we take this major chord form and add three notes just below it at the second fret, we have the basis for the "road map" to the banjo neck. **(Ex. 2)** These notes are probably familiar because they are used as "slides" and "hammer-ons" when playing bluegrass banjo. Most bluegrass banjo consists of G major chord tones plus these three added notes which emphasis the melody. This is the amazing thing about the addition to the basic G chord: You can build a system which will produce both major and minor sounds! And what's more it's a snap to learn! It's like getting a musical "two-for-one" deal.

The first part of this book involves becoming familiar with the "sonic shapes" like the one above. One can only expand sound perception by playing. This is the real purpose of this book. Remember that the idea here is not to focus on theory, but on sound. Always ask yourself what it means in sound. Now that you know a major sound can also imply a minor sound, we can begin to explore fingerings in both the single string and arpa techniques.

About Right and Left Hand Technique

Some of the growing pains of the five string's current popularity center around allegiances to one technique or another. Finger rolls are very popular nowadays. Most players "pluck" the same string many times in a row by alternating thumb and index. Some may even alternate thumb and middle. There are players who use the classical right hand technique of alternating the index and middle fingers of their right hand. It is entirely up to you. You may pluck in the manner in which you are most comfortable. Except for a few cases, this book will be purposely generic in regards to technique. It is basically your choice. There are plenty of great books on technique. Besides, you have more than likely formed your own habits already.

The chord form above is built on a pentatonic scale. "Pentatonic" means five tones. Both chords, G major and E minor, can be painted by the G pentatonic scale if care is given to proper emphasis on chord tones. The emphasis on chord tones is the only difference! Why? See the Practical Theory Appendix, p. 48.

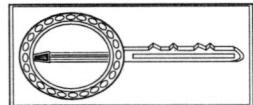

The Key To Five String Banjo

It is beneficial to anchor the right hand ring or little finger (or both) on the banjo head. If the index and thumb are used to play single-string passages, then play each of the exercises in this book starting first with the index, and then with the thumb. If you find that you cannot increase your speed, then you may want to consider changing your right hand technique for more efficiency.

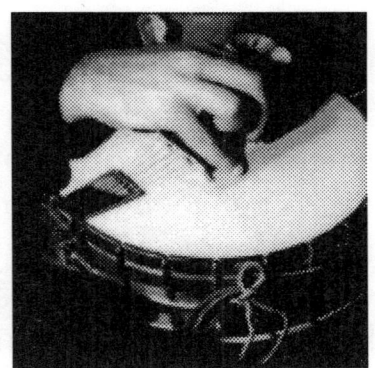

Choice of left hand technique is a matter of personal preference. Many rest the palm of the hand on the back of the banjo neck. A few use the classical technique of placing only the thumb behind the neck. I personally use the latter because I have found that it gives me a better mechanical advantage over the strings. It also allows me to avoid the fifth string peg (which gets in the way when you "palm" the neck). You will probably find that many of the upcoming exercises will stretch your left hand. Placing the thumb behind the neck will make it easier to complete these exercises.

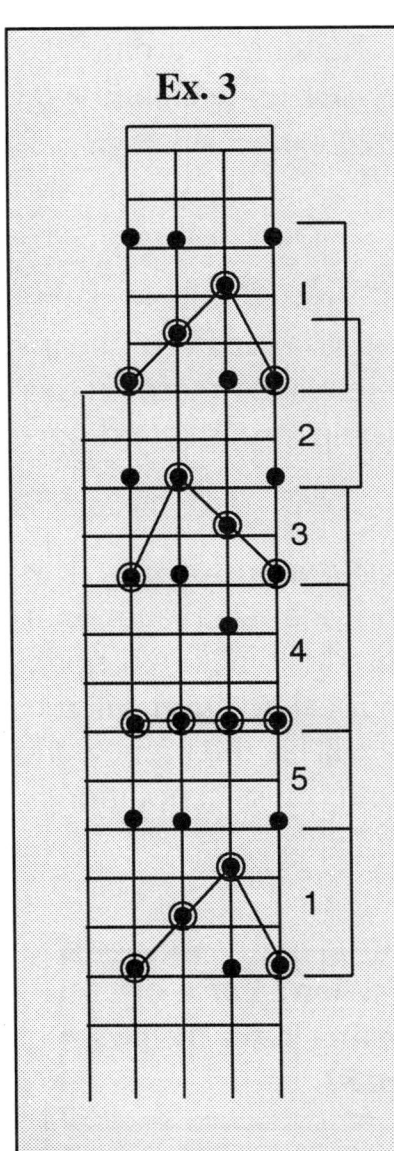

Two Kinds of Chords - One System

When you take these five notes and spread them down the entire fretboard, the following pattern is created. (**Ex. 3**) The neck is divided into five different areas of activity. Learning these areas one at a time increases your control of the neck. These patterns are numbered and the basic major chord tones are circled.

It is a great way to learn the neck because the system is easily adapted for use against any chord type. When its potential is realized, the range of the entire fretboard materializes with a minimum amount of practice!

The greatest thing about the grid on the left is that it is at once both a *G major* **and** *E minor* pattern. A major chord can be thought of as a different kind of minor chord! OK. So what does this mean practically?

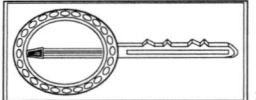

The Key To Five String Banjo

It means that when either a G or Em chord is sounded by a rhythm instrument, you can play any combination of the notes in **(Ex. 3)** without playing a "wrong" note! Imagine that! You can freely improvise with the notes on this grid while the guitar toggles between G major and E minor chords! It is not even necessary to know when the guitar is going to change chords. You may not be playing great licks, but the notes will not clash with a G major or an E minor chord. The letter of the chord changes but the chord form and sounds are identical! This basic form generates very logical patterns. You simply have to train your fingers and ears to hear them. You learn major as a different kind of minor. (See What *Is Improvisation* below)

So why in the world would you want to learn this? The basic idea is to become aware of where you are on the neck first. Great licks will come later! After decades of practice and stage experience, this template and the associated chord forms will be perceived unconsciously and probably in fragmented form. Therefore, learning this simple grid consciously and completely can only accelerate your understanding of how the neck is structured, thus saving years of hit or miss practice.

Summary

The idea is to transfer sound in your head to a "left hand" consciousness in the least amount of time. In essence, for the gentle art of improvisation, you "hear" through your left hand. Bet you didn't know it had ears! There will be more on this later. A recording is provided with all the exercises and will help in this sound perception goal.

Almost all the exercises include musical notation. There is a reason for this. The debate about whether tab can suffice for musical notation and vice versa rages on. I neither endorse nor oppose any causes in this regard. I figured if I included both, then you will get the best of both worlds and maybe some musical notation will rub off on you. Tab is necessary at first to impart fingerings which will lay the framework for the road map or "Key" on the fretboard. On the other hand, musical notation is the standard for the music world.

 **What are the basic concepts behind improvisation? For a brief outline of what it is and how you can start learning it, see the jazz improvisation section in the Jazz Appendix, p. 52.**

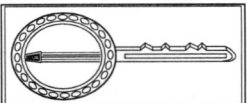

The Key To Five String Banjo

Into Action!

" He who has begun his task has half done it. Have
the courage to be wise; Begin!"
                       Horace, Epistles (13 B.C.)

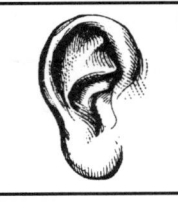 **So here we go! Each position is demonstrated with closed fingerings and then with alternate open string fingerings. Listen to position #1 on the recording FIRST, hum it as a "mini-tune", THEN play the tab.**

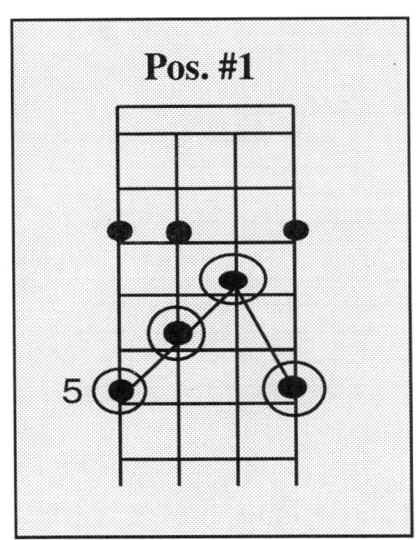

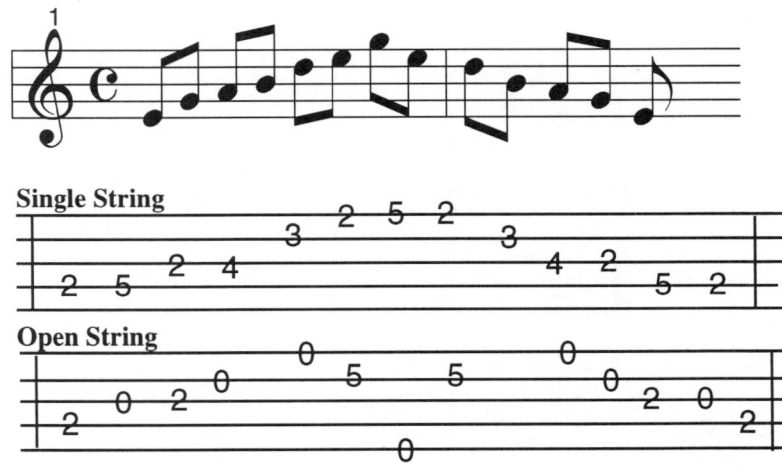

Now stop the recording and play it slowly. Keep in mind that this is both a G major and an E minor sound. The guitar on the recording plays both G major and E minor behind each exercise. As you read the tabulature, try to relate to the notes on the music staff. Always start slowly and feel your fingers slowly getting familiar with the pattern. When you feel fairly comfortable with it, try closing your eyes as you play, visualizing your left hand. This visualization process is very important. If you cannot find the notes with your eyes closed, then go back to the tab and music until you have the position under your fingers. Then, close your eyes or turn your head away from the tab and try it again. Under the musical notation are both single string and alternate open string configurations.

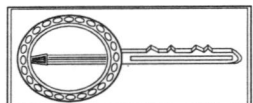

The Key To Five String Banjo

This first position will stretch your left hand so that you get practice with the little finger. The first note of the exercise is played with the index finger of the left hand and the second note with the little finger. For this first position, each fret from the second to the fifth uses a specific finger from the left hand. In other words, a note fretted at the second fret uses the index, the third fret uses the middle, a note fretted at the fourth fret the ring finger and fifth fret uses the little finger-A FINGER FOR EACH FRET!

Spend about 10 minutes playing position #1 up and down, then move to position #2 and utilize the same process of visualization and hand-to-ear coordination. Remember to listen to the recording first!

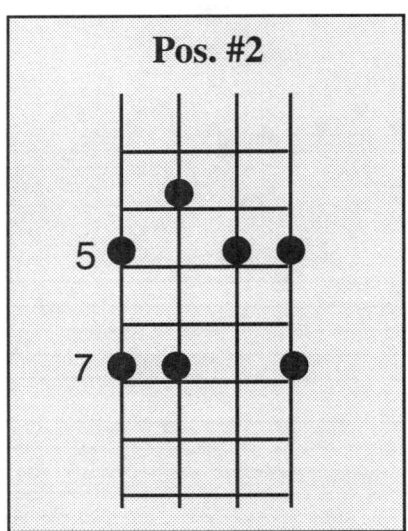
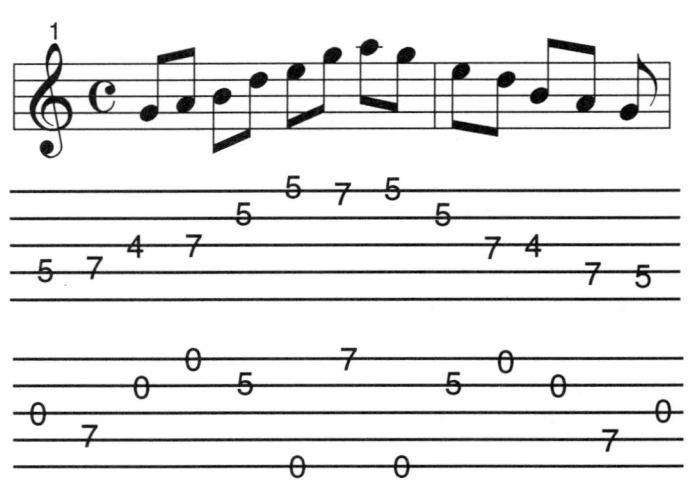

The 2nd position, and the 4th position above are transitions. They lie between the 1st, 3rd and 5th positions which outline major chords (circled notes).

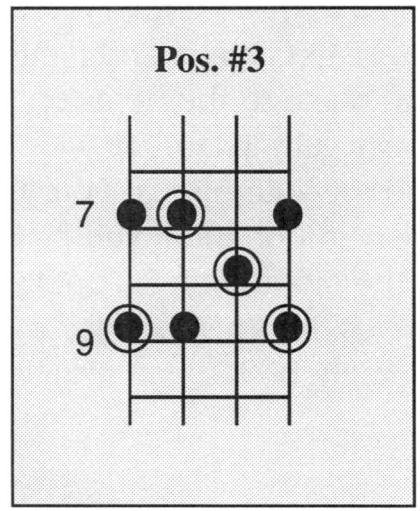
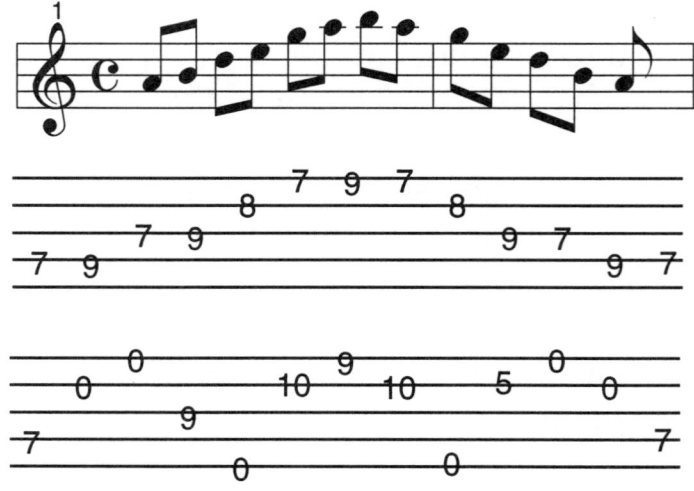

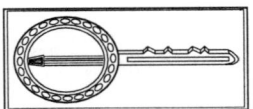

The Key To Five String Banjo

Remember that you are adding new habit patterns. Always "think" G major and E minor as you play these positions. Think of this grid as an "overview" from which to draw musical ideas. In time, it will become ingrained.

The fourth position includes the bar G formation at the twelfth fret.

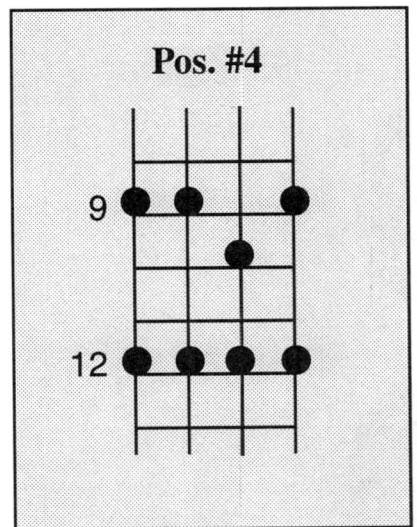
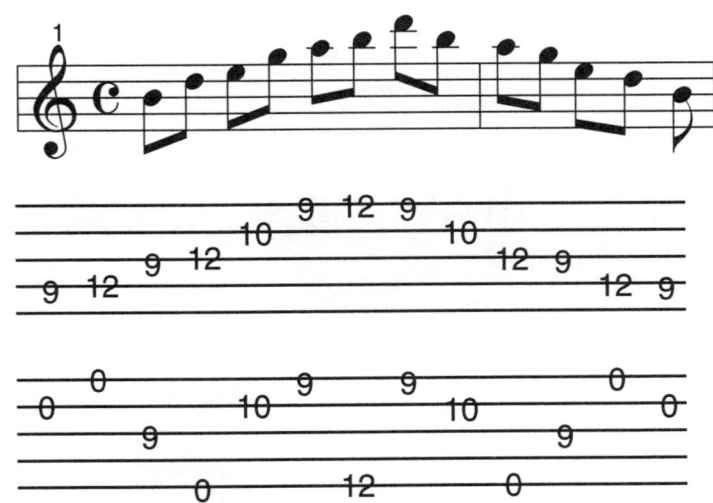

Below the 12th fret, the fifth position is actually the bar formation plus the three added notes we started with. These are the same three notes added at the second fret to form the first position. The whole pattern then repeats at the 17th fret completing the grid. **(see Ex. 3, p. 15)**

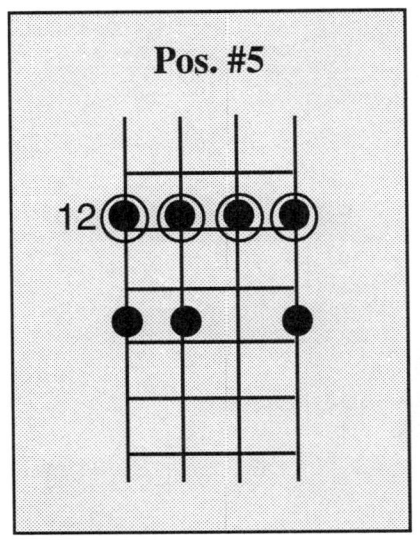
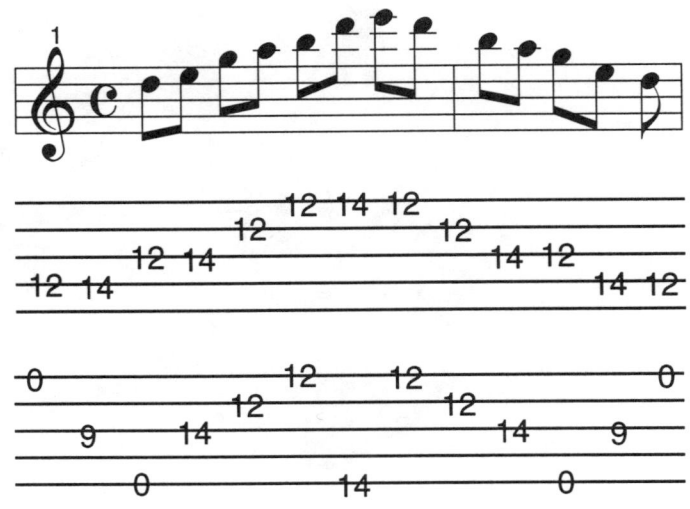

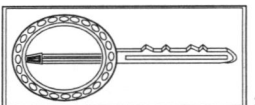

The Key To Five String Banjo

Exercises

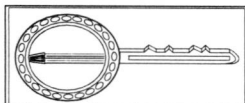 The Key To Five String Banjo

Now Hear This!

The exercises that follow will help the student internalize the five positions shown previously. But that is not the primary goal. This selection of exercises could well be termed "ear to hand training." The goal is not to learn new licks but to enhance your conception of the fretboard and prepare you for the realm of improvisation. They will improve visual as well as your aural awareness. The following patterns are designed to help you learn the neck of the banjo while also increasing your dexterity.

Changing one's perception can be a slow process partially because we tend to cling to old habit-patterns unconsciously. In improvisation, all attention is on the left hand in an actual playing situation. It seems as though the left hand has ears and searches for sounds. When playing, attention focuses on the left hand and the right hand subconsciously follows. The left hand leads and the right hand follows. The quicker you relinquish your dependence on the tab, the faster your left hand will progress.

It should be pointed out that practice is a totally different realm than performing. Everything learned in practice has to be under your fingers, COLD. Practice is the awareness of your fingering, the chord you are on, timing and any other elements which are necessary to prepare you for playing with others. Performing, as opposed to practice, is not so much thinking. The closest thing to describing what happens when you perform is that there is a world of sound and your left hand. The player is mostly interested in shaping a solo inside a rhythmic framework. I've heard it described as a kind of relaxed, detached maintenance in which you are the listener as well as the player.

 **Practicing is always knowing where you are musically. What's the easiest way to go about learning the notes on a banjo neck? See the Theory Appendix on page 50 to get started.**

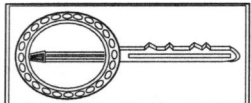

The Key To Five String Banjo

G/Em Exercises

Preparing for Practice

✔   The basic approach starts with sound. Listen to the recording first. If you have a tape player in your car, you might listen to the exercises and learn them as you drive. Use the instrument you have the closest relationship to - your voice. Match the taped examples by singing or simply humming them **BEFORE** playing the tab. Learn each exercise as a mini-song.

✔   The next step is to transfer what you have learned by ear to the banjo via your left hand. Read the tab as you simultaneously hum the exercise. Use sound to teach your left hand. Then play the example while looking at your left hand, not the tab.

✔   Everything bows down to repetition. In order to go fast, go slowly! Build a little at a time, repeating from the beginning while adding notes until you can play the whole line. Don't bite off more than you can chew. The idea is to try to feel where a pattern connects. The recording will give you an idea of how these patterns sound in G/Em.

✔   The basic rule for both right and left hand fingering is to have a finger ready, anticipating each upcoming note. If the fingering is too awkward, you will know soon enough because it will be difficult to gain speed.

In examples #1 through #6, each closed position or single string pattern can be reversed by simply reading it backwards from right-to-left. Single string closed patterns can be visualized around geometric shapes on the fretboard. A pattern can ascend or descend in pitch and in position as it progresses up or down the neck. You are encouraged to play a "mirror image" of each pattern. Always start slowly and increase speed on each exercise only when you are absolutely sure you are using the correct fingers. There should be "daylight" between each note!

Corrections to KTFSB

Page 23 - Ex. #2

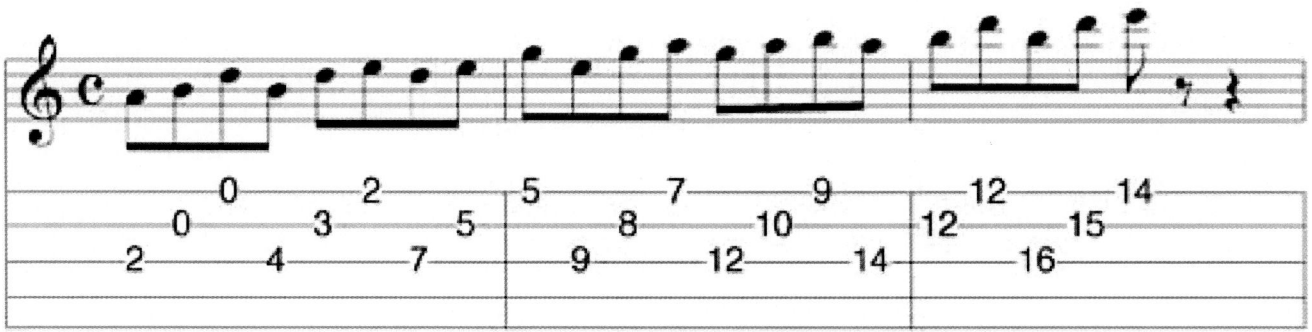

Page 23 - Ex. #4

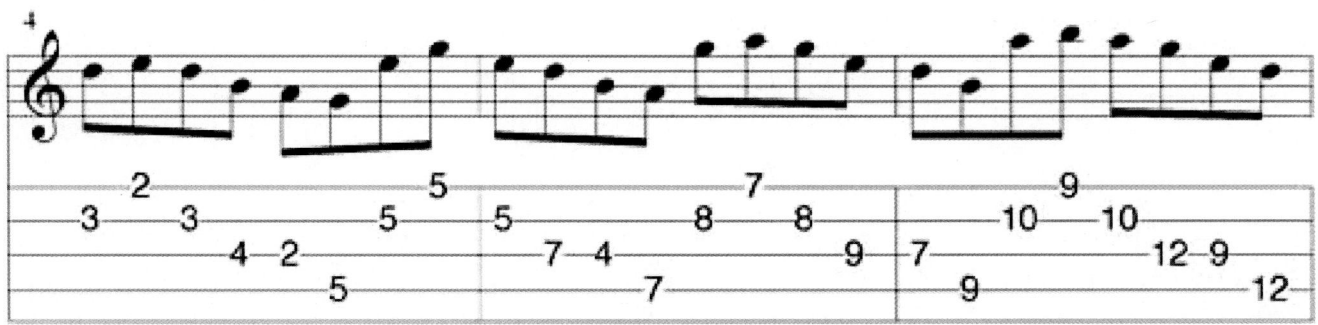

Page 25 - Ex. #9

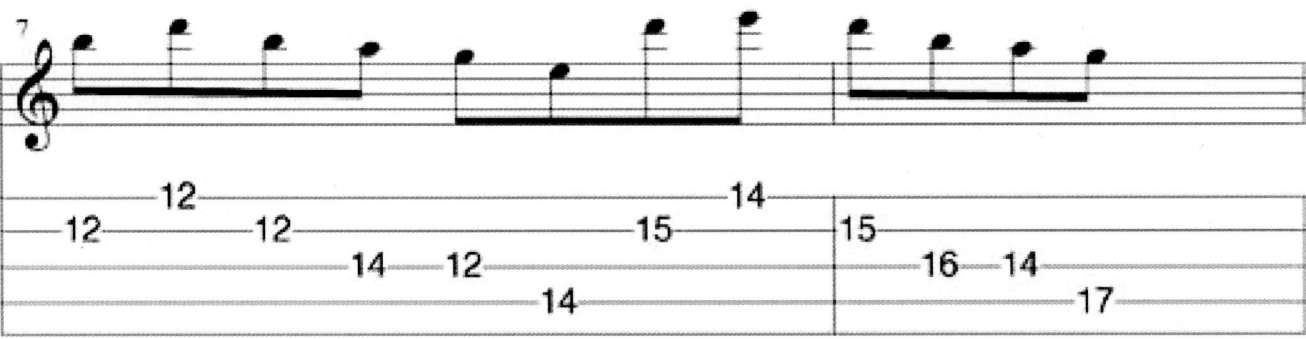

Key of E♭
"Banjo Tuned Low"
I.

LORENA

Arranged by
John Hartford

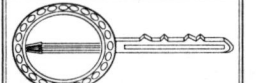

The Key To Five String Banjo

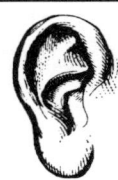

Here are six exercises based upon the previously outlined five key positions. Again, the recording will guide you. Always rely on the sound - not on tablature!

1

2

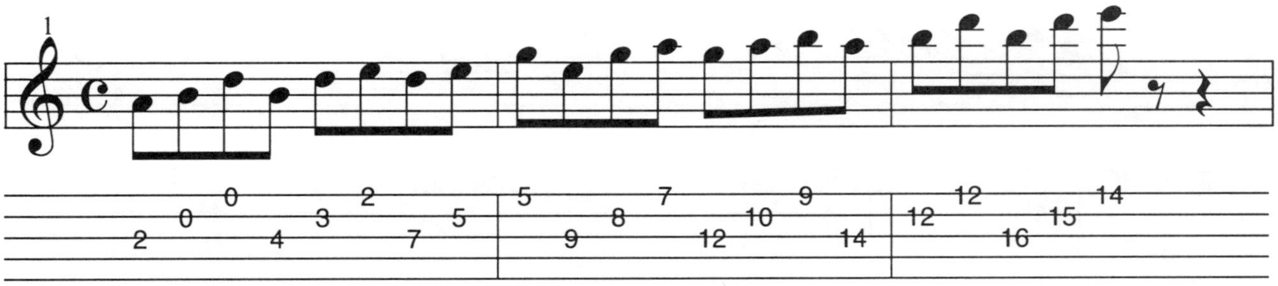

3

4

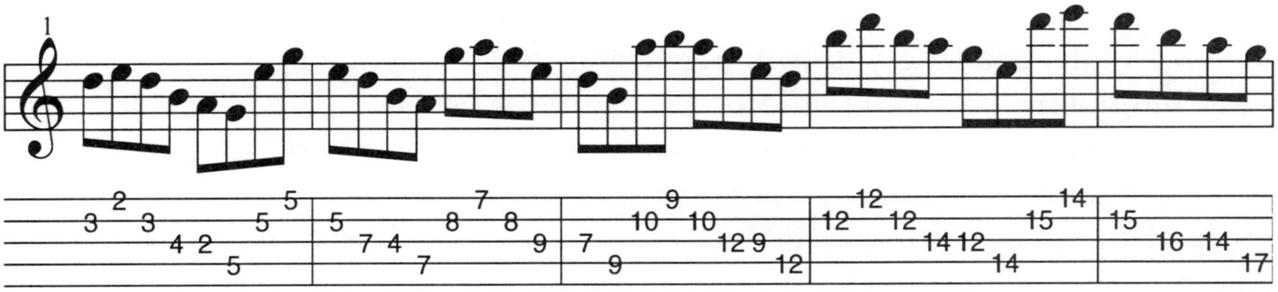

23

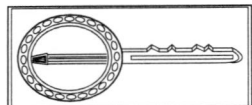 **The Key To Five String Banjo**

Pattern #5 utilizes the 4th, 3rd and 2nd strings and pattern #6, uses the first three strings only. You can also reverse and mirror image any of these to challenge your fingers.

#5
2nd, 3rd & 4th strings

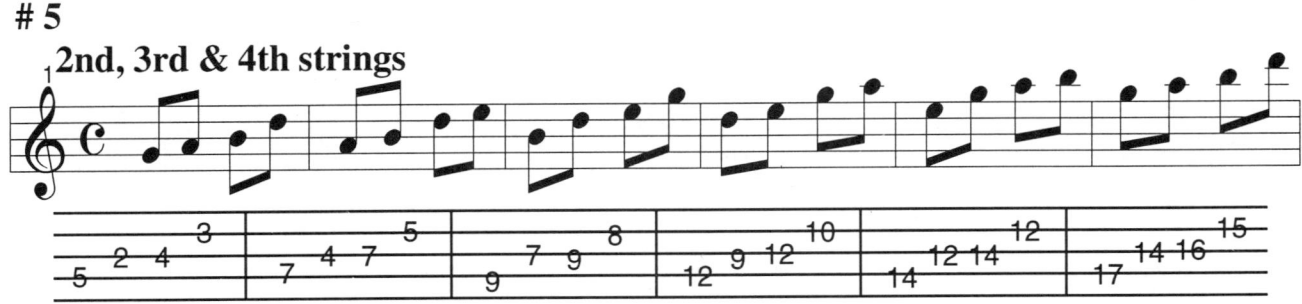

#6
3rd, 2nd & 1st strings

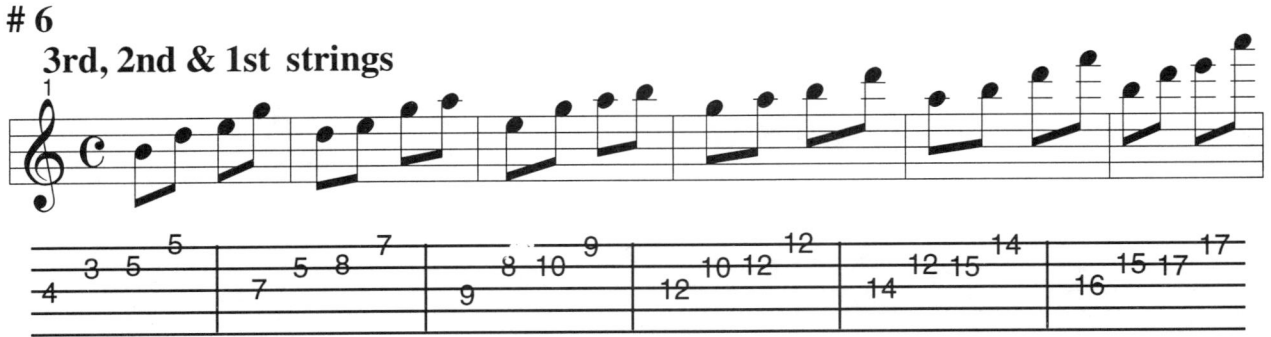

Open String Exercises

Five-string banjo is a unique musical invention. Because of its standard tuning (G) there are possibilities for "across string" or arpa (harp) style (sometimes known by the misnomer "melodic style") which includes the fifth string. This kind of playing is different - it is more abstract. It relies on open strings to allow your left hand to shift to different locations on the fretboard. It includes special case situations which are unique to each key.

Open string fingerings provide an opportunity from having to hold a string or position down, thus enabling you to move to the next sequence in a pattern. Many times, infrequent use of the little finger can be a problem. See that this weakest finger gets exercised! If a smooth sound isn't obtained at first, keep trying. Always! If it absolutely feels so awkward that you almost consider taking up accordion, then by all means go back and rethink your approach, making sure to have a finger ready for each new move. Don't be afraid to experiment in order to remedy awkward fingerings.

The Key To Five String Banjo

Patterns using open strings (melodic style) are intriguing to learn because they rely more on sound instinct to determine where an open string fits in. The right hand fingering is also less apparent. Therefore, the sound of the pattern becomes the important aid in learning the fingering. Can you sing or whistle the notes you are trying to find? The sound must carry you through because the visualizations that partially guided you in the closed positions are absent.

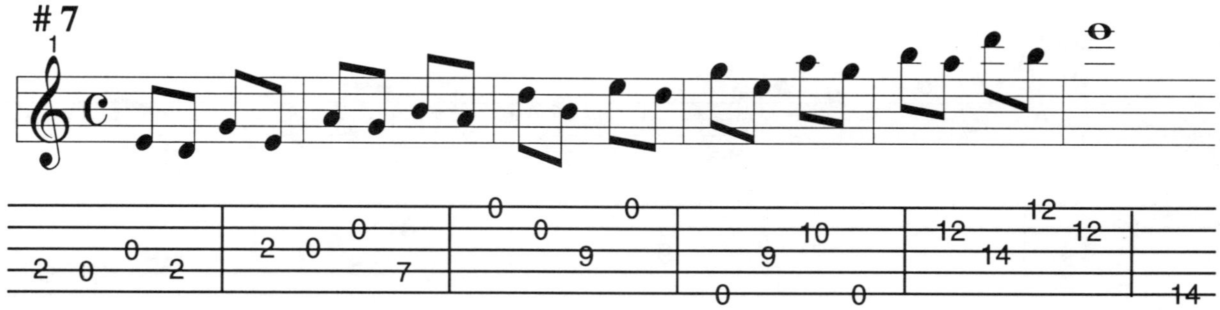

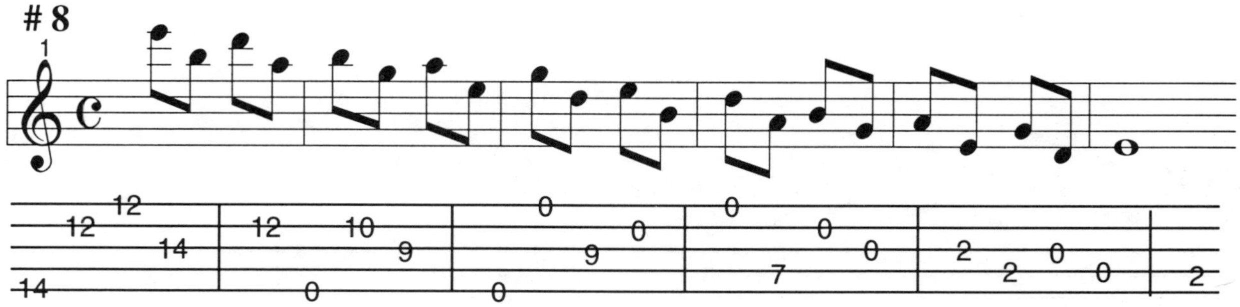

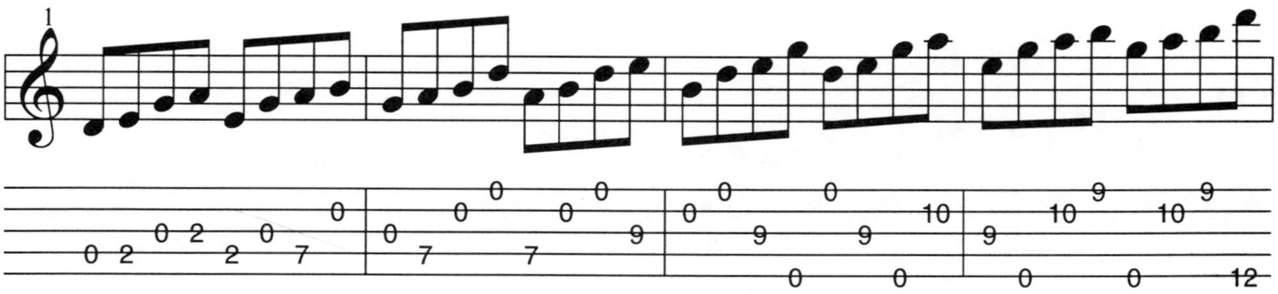

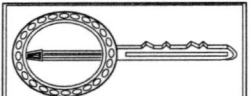

The Key To Five String Banjo

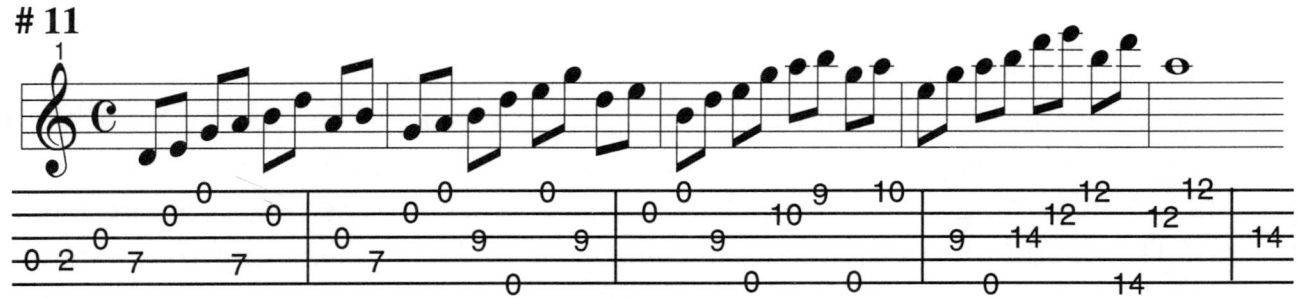

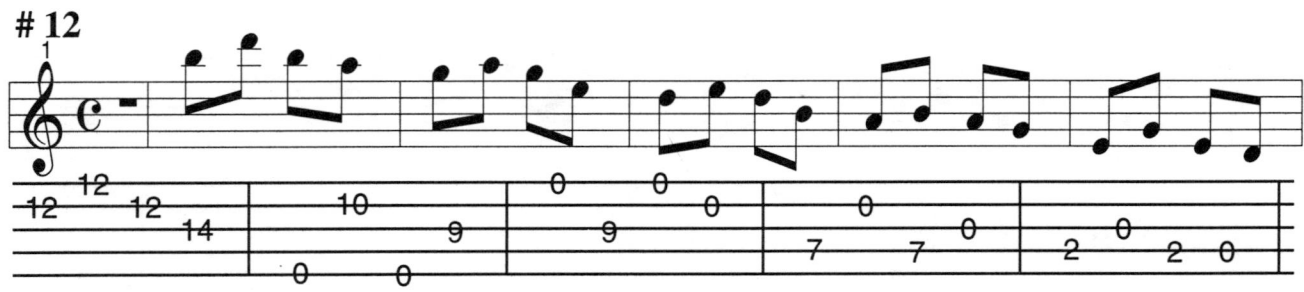

These exercises outline areas from which you may later draw musical ideas. Think of it as a training or preparation for things to come. Eventually, you will be able to discern how chords or phrases fit into the whole picture.

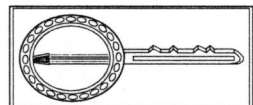

The Key To Five String Banjo

The following studies make use of the formula of playing up three notes in each position and falling back to the original starting note. The last two notes of each bar when played consecutively result in the interval pattern.

Interval Studies

Pos. #1

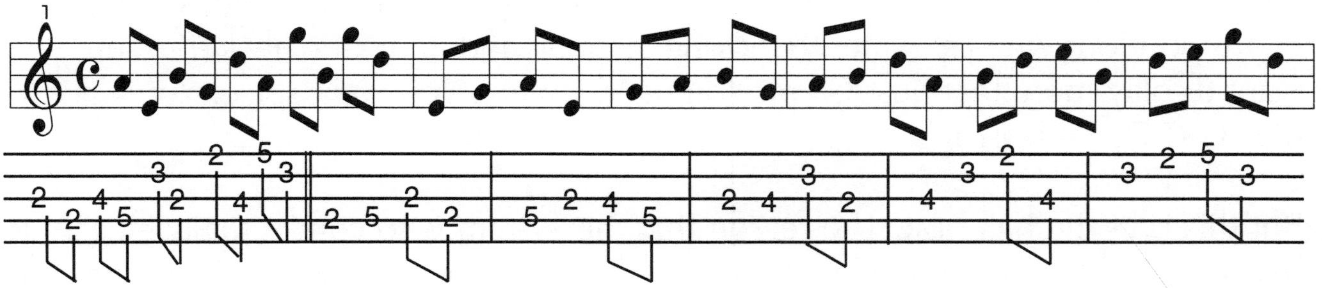

Pos. #2

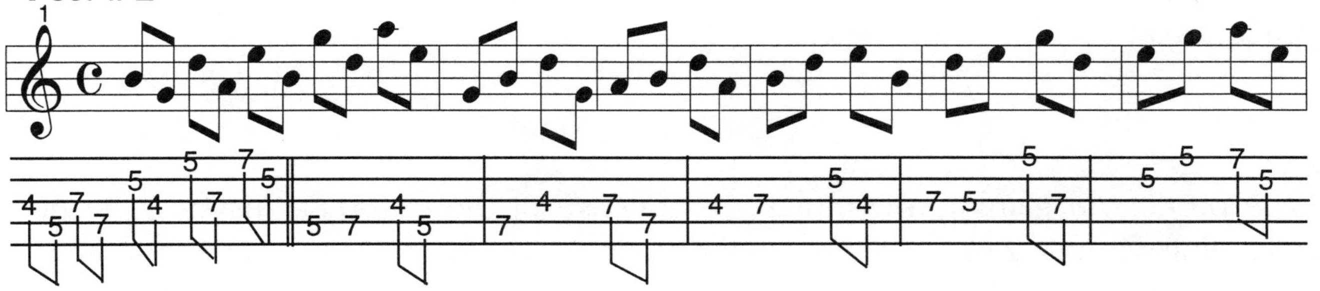

Pos. #3

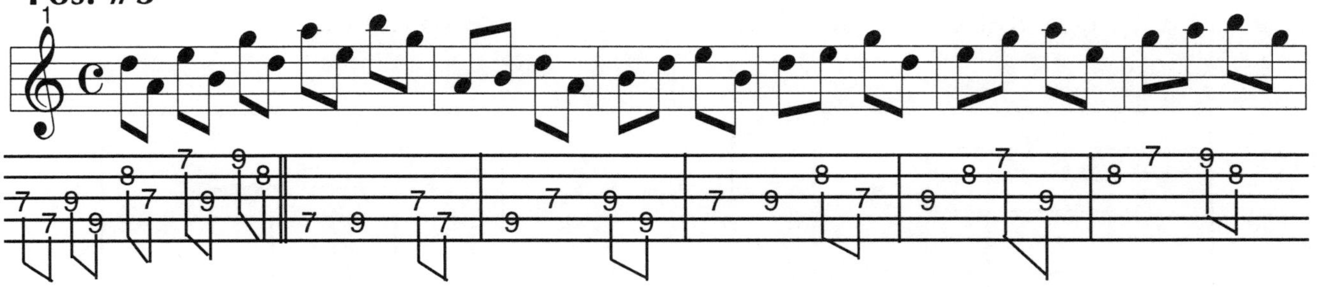

Pos. #4

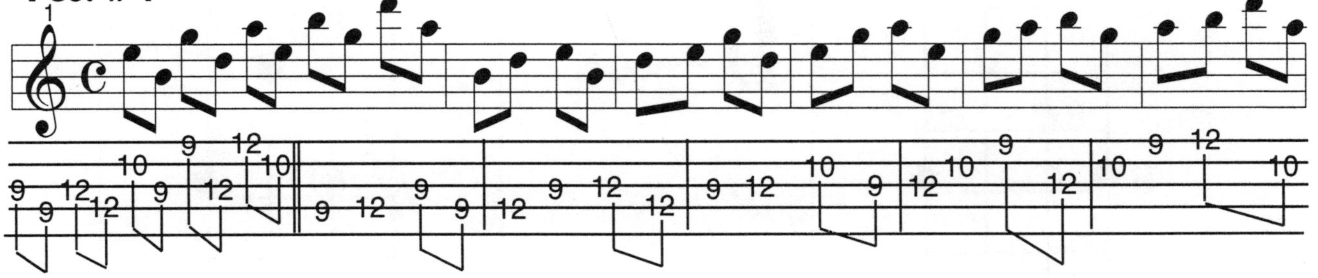

Pos. #5

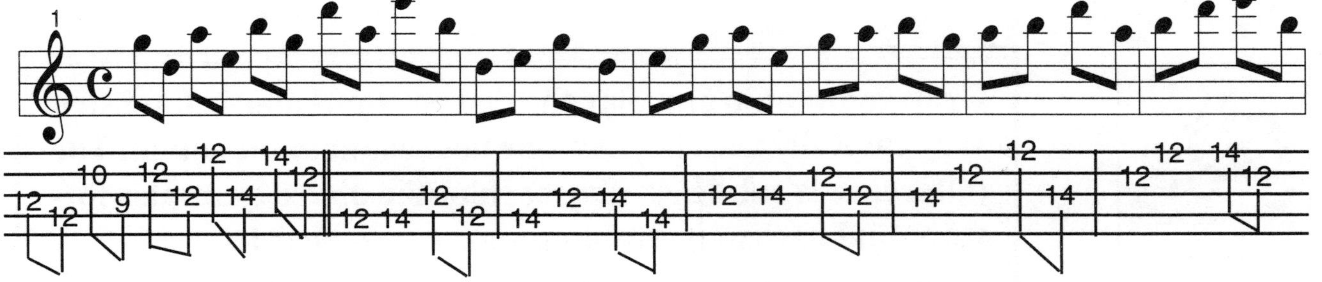

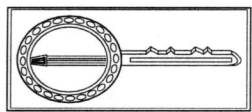

The Key To Five String Banjo

Position Shifts

OK! Now here's where it really gets good. You might be thinking, "If these positions give you G/Em then moving any of them up 5 frets will give me C/Am, right?" The answer is of course: Yes! These pentatonic positions are just like your basic major chord positions when it comes to moving them up and down the neck. I'm sure you want to play more than just G/Em! You need variety. You want spice. You want to play G-C-D! (At least!)

But this isn't the half of it. The reason that this system is so conceptually elegant is because you can alter a single position on the fretboard to play a basic progression like G-C-D. We can begin with the first of the five G/Em positions introduced a few pages ago.

Change One Note!

The process of gaining a complete perspective of the fretboard involves position changing within a 2 or 4 fret area. In the example below, the basic G/Em pentatonic position is changed to C/Am by altering just one note! You change the "B" note by moving it up one fret to "C" and Pos. #1 (G/Em) turns to (C/Am).

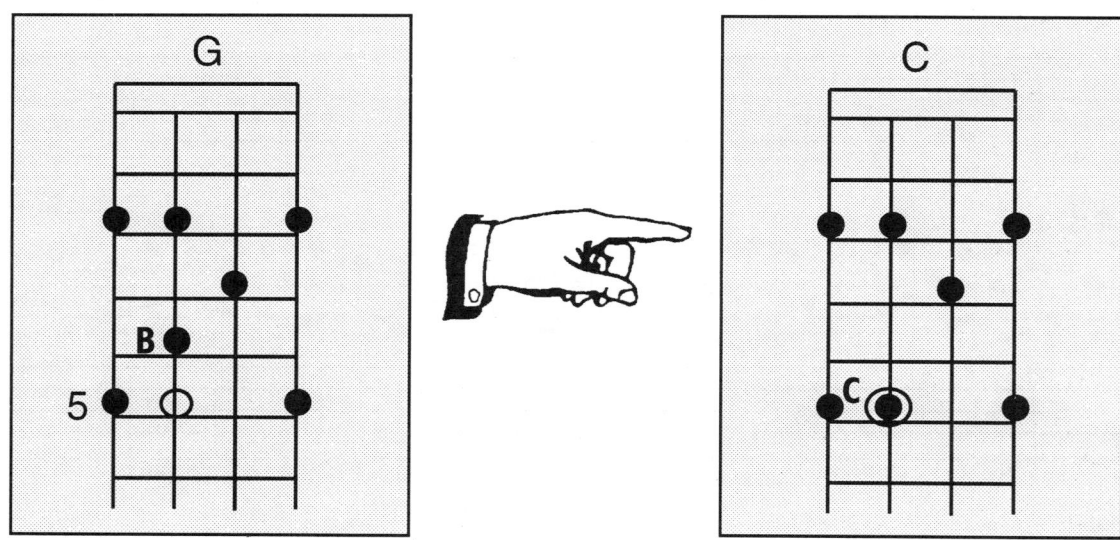

> **Grab your banjo and play the two positions above and listen very carefully noticing how one note changes the sound. The difference is subtle, so play each of the above examples forward and backward training your ear to hear it.**

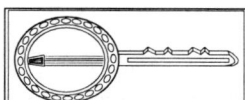

The Key To Five String Banjo

The effect of changing a "B" note to "C" is to move the whole position up five frets. Each of the remaining four G/Em pentatonic positions are altered to C/Am by simply changing one note. Note that all positions follow symmetrically. Changing chords in one position is a good way to learn chord progressions. It helps keep you in the same area of the neck. In an actual playing situation, when you feel a chord change from G to C, the perception of when the chord will change is anticipated. After some practice, it becomes automatic. Thus, every G position is only one note away from being a C position.

Learning how to handle many different chord progressions is the eventual goal. The previous exercises for G/Em can also be applied to the C/Am and the D/Bm positions. Think of both major and minor for each chord type as you practice them. All positions and chords are linked and never change order. The examples show how the "B" note in every position can be moved up one fret to "C", thus making the whole position reflect a C/Am kind of sound. Learning to change chords by position shifts will enable you to feel at home wherever you are on the neck. You will anticipate a chord change while creating and shaping melodies as you go - and that's not all.

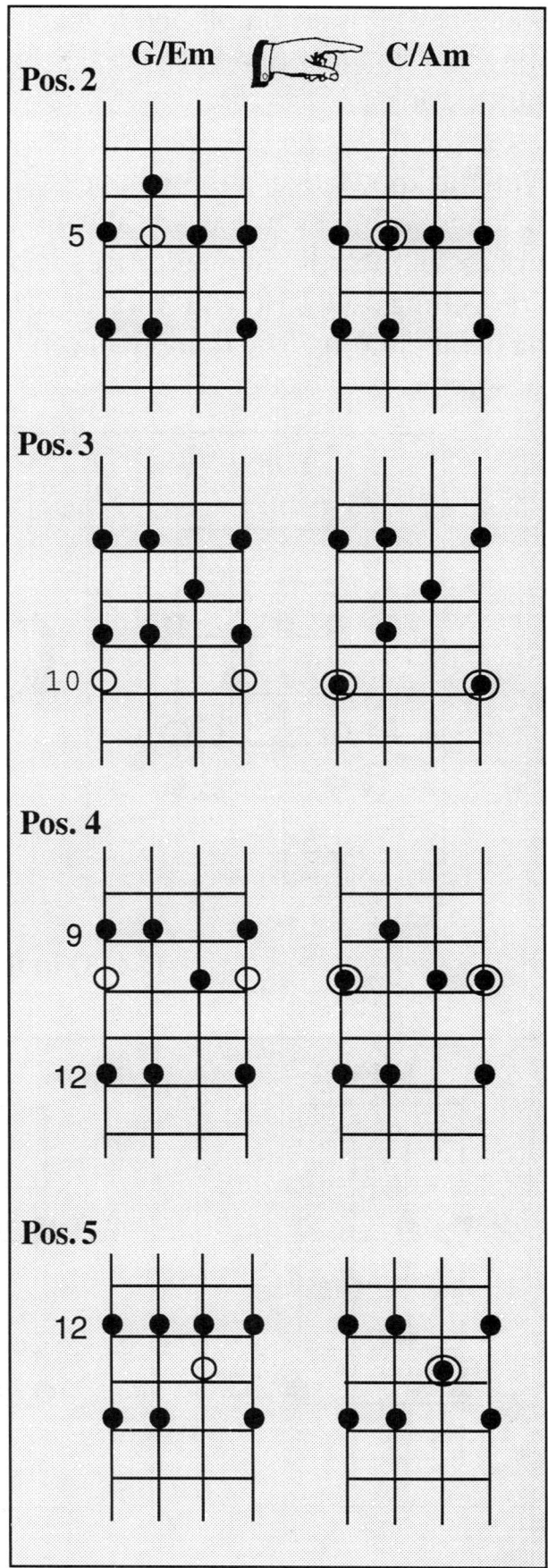

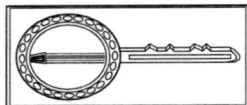

The Key To Five String Banjo

The same process can be applied to change from the G/Em position to the D/Bm position. This is accomplished in each of the G/Em positions by simply flatting (lowering) the "G" note one fret to "F#". Simply lower the "G" note on both the first and fourth strings.

With the knowledge of these basic G, C, and D positions, you can construct patterns to songs with which you are already familiar and modify your current solos. The process of melody shaping proceeds by awkward trial and error at first. However, after getting used to it, you will start to enjoy the satisfaction of acquiring new fingering habit patterns. The things you can hear will start to command your fingers. Now for some G-C-D exercises!

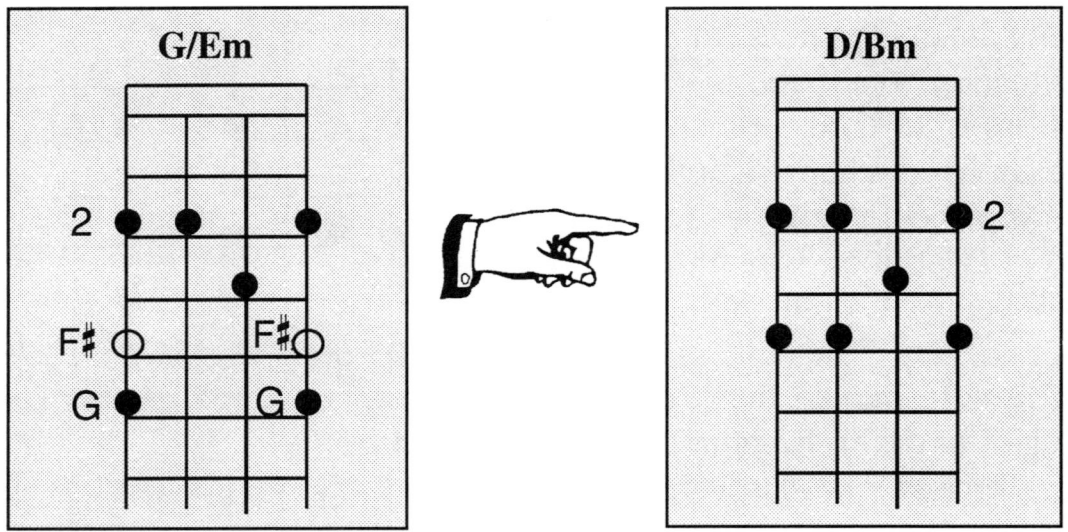

G-C-D in the first position:

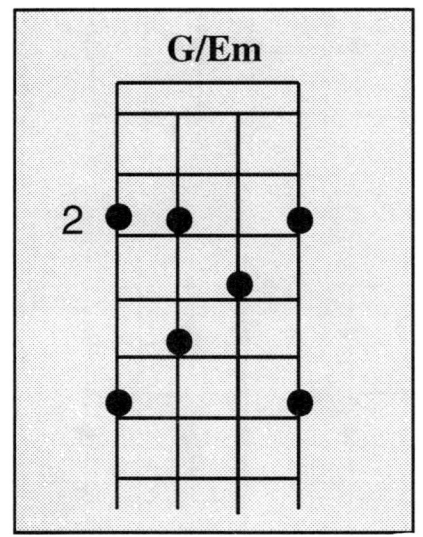
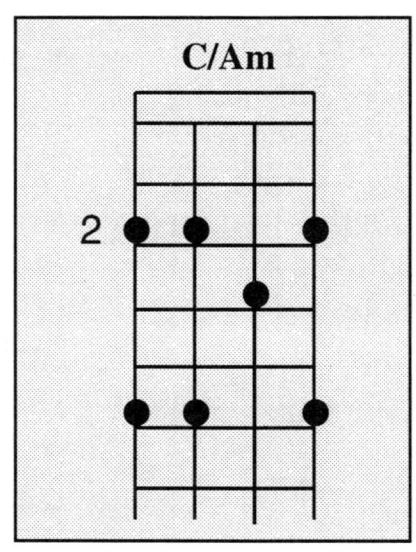
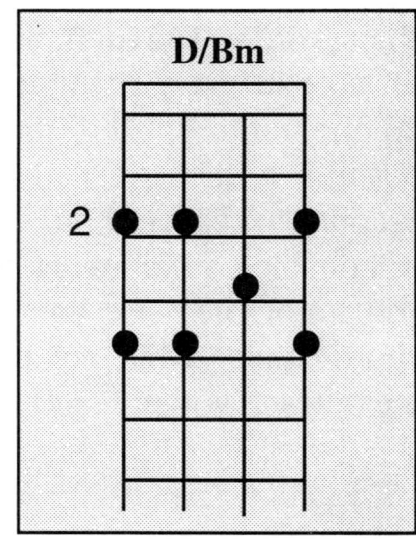

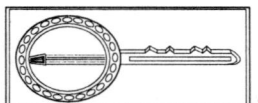

Exercises for G-C-D

Closed Positions:

Pos. # 1

Pos. # 2

Pos. # 3

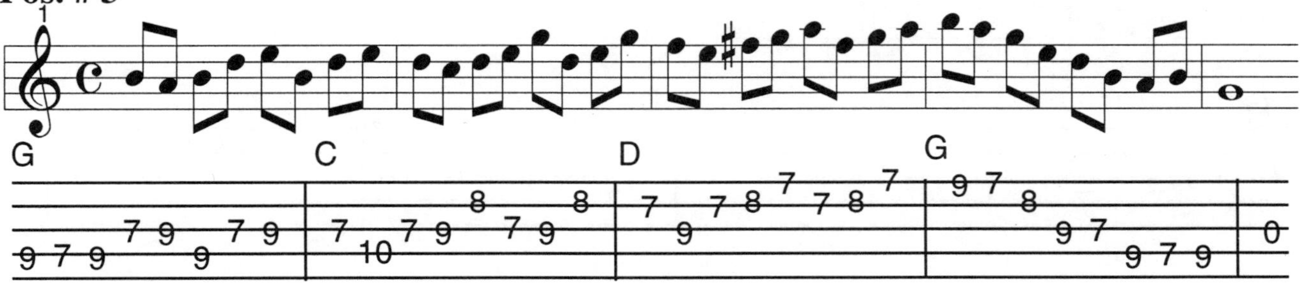

Pos. # 4

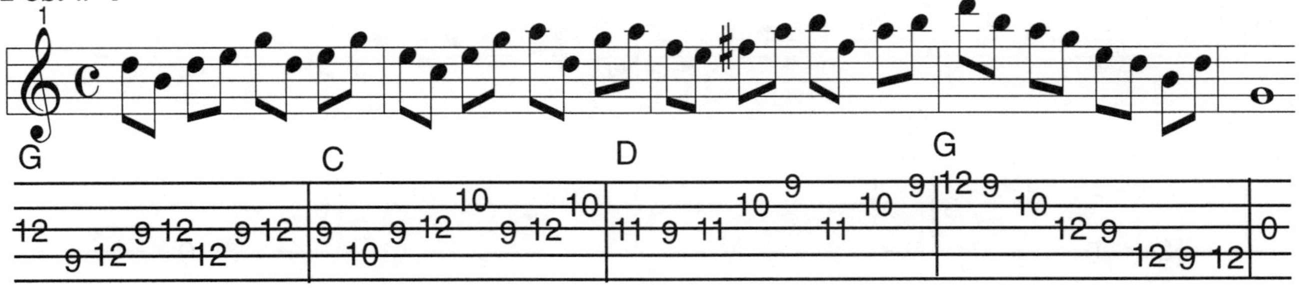

Pos. # 5

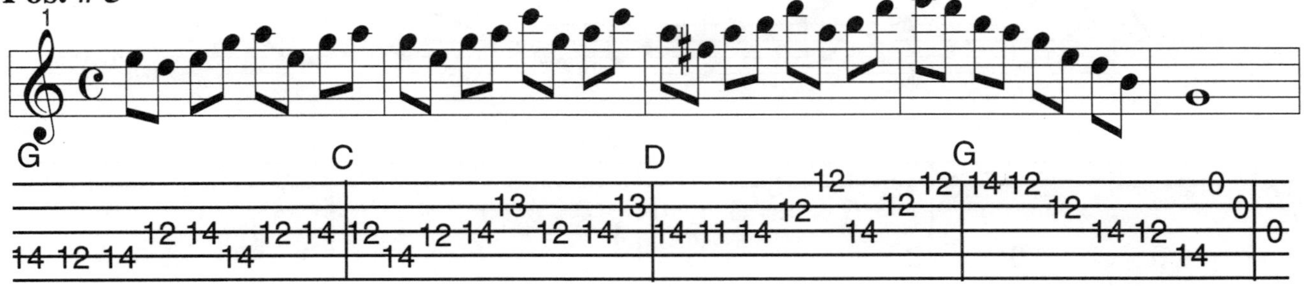

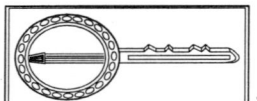

The Key To Five String Banjo

Open fingerings

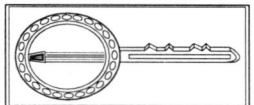

The Key To Five String Banjo

While position shifts help your concept in a single area of the neck, playing the full range of G-C-D with pentatonic scales completes the full view of the neck in sound. It is important to get practice throughout the range of the instrument in G, C and D pentatonic scales.

G/Em
G-A-B-D-E

C-Am
C-D-E-G-A

D/Bm
G-A-B-D-E

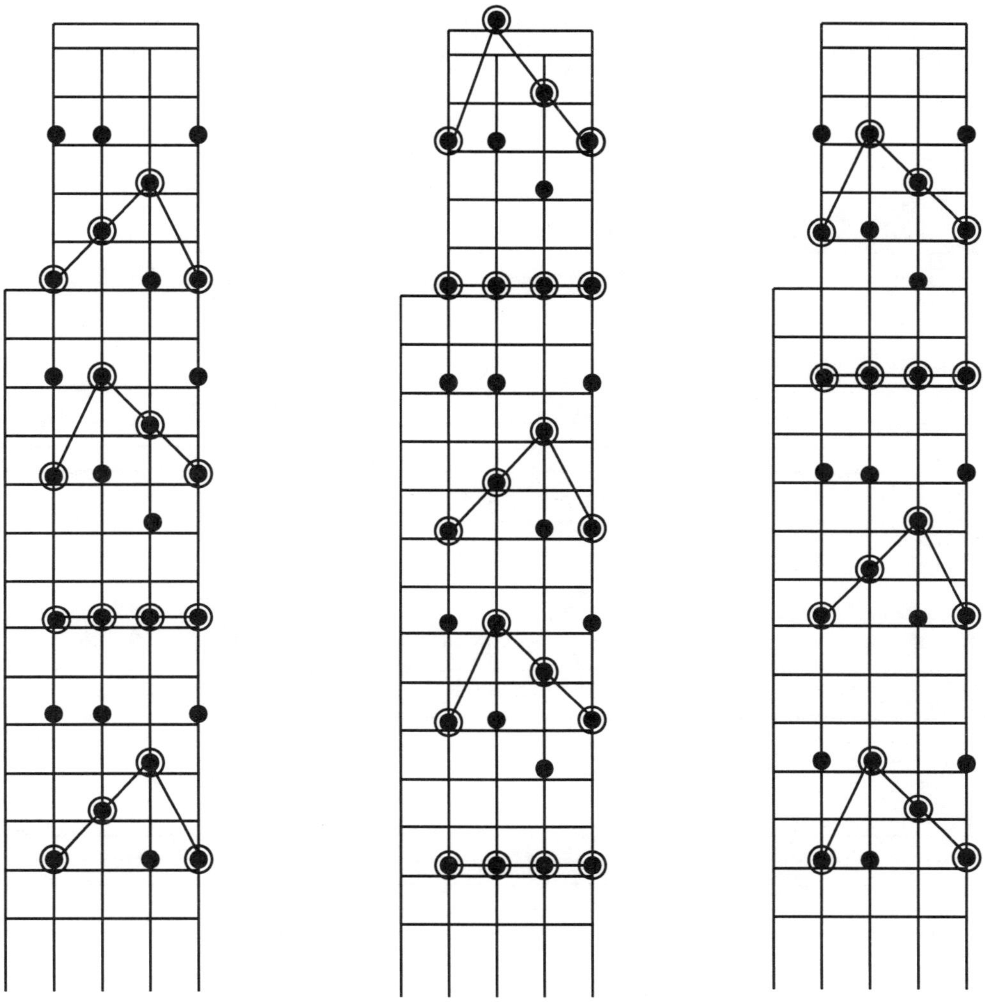

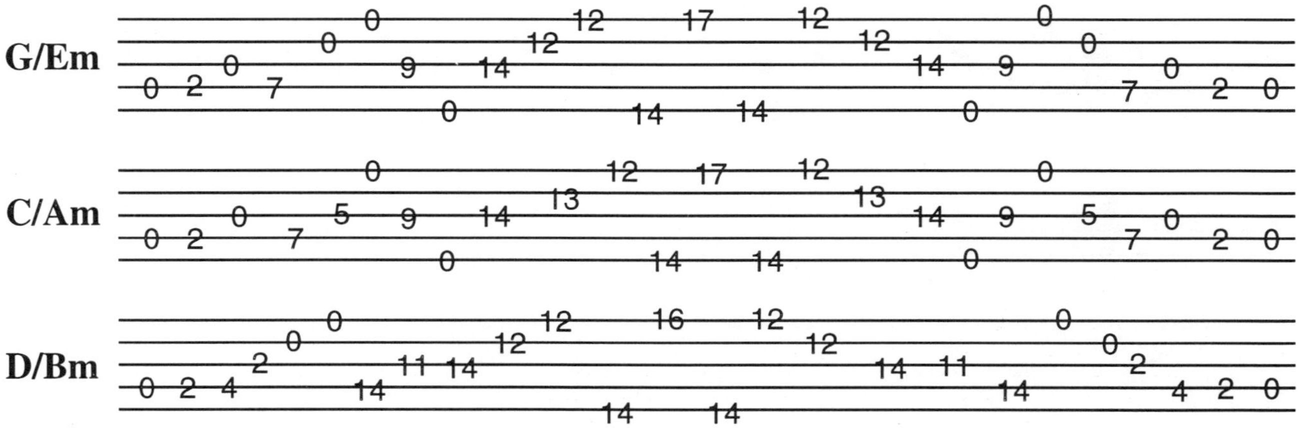

33

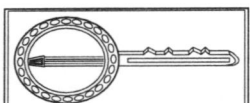

The Key To Five String Banjo

Song Study: Sally Johnson

Fiddle tunes are fun to learn and can demonstrate the five Key Positions. The fiddle tune Sally Johnson is a good example. It shows how closed positions work and how the neck is structured. This song is played entirely in closed position utilizing three of the previously demonstrated pentatonic positions. The song starts at the 4 position just above the bar G chord at the twelfth fret. In the sixth measure, a move from the 4 position to the 3 position occurs and is followed by a shift to the 1 position in part B:

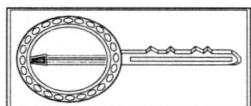

The Key To Five String Banjo

Closed positions make it possible for you to play this tune in other keys simply by moving all the fingerings up or down the neck. Try the song moved up two frets to the key of A or down two frets to the key of F.

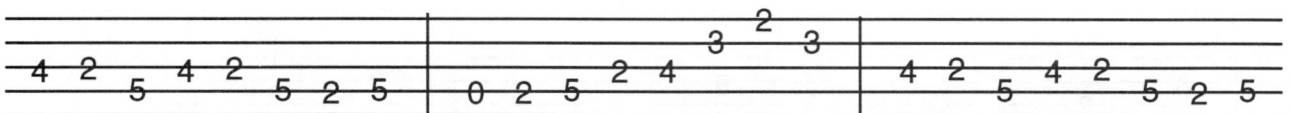

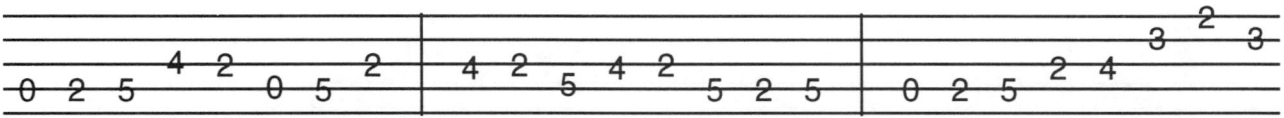

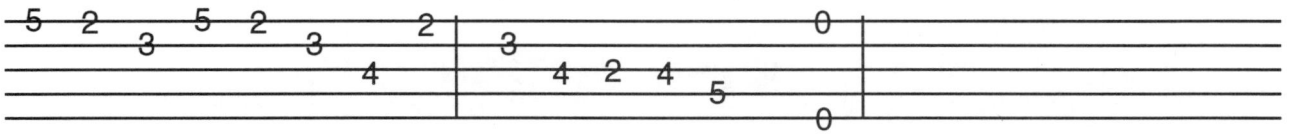

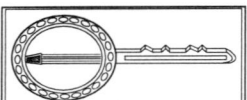

The Key To Five String Banjo

Melodic Fingering

An alternate fingering in the "across string" style is quite different in its phrasing. Arpa style utilizes open strings, giving a different feel to the way the notes are perceived. The difference, though subtle, produces nuances in phrasing which is more legato or smooth.

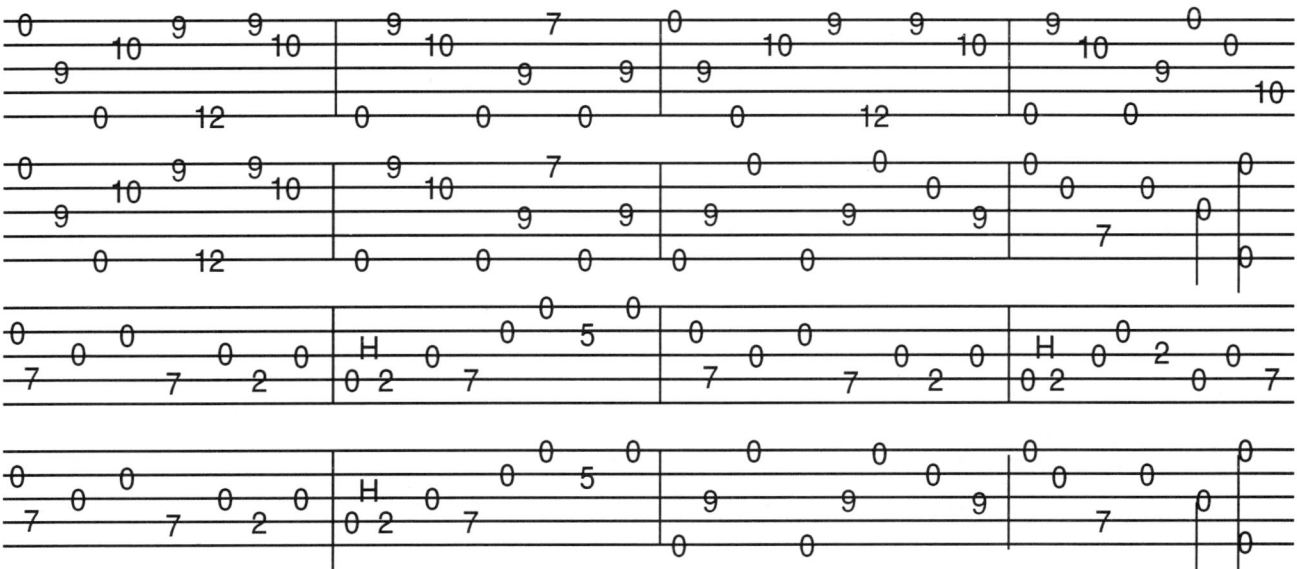

The last example shows fingering with embellishments. These notes, which are neither pentatonic nor major scale notes, add interest by providing tension within the melody. They usually precede a melody note or are one fret higher or lower than the original melody note or chord tone (arrows):

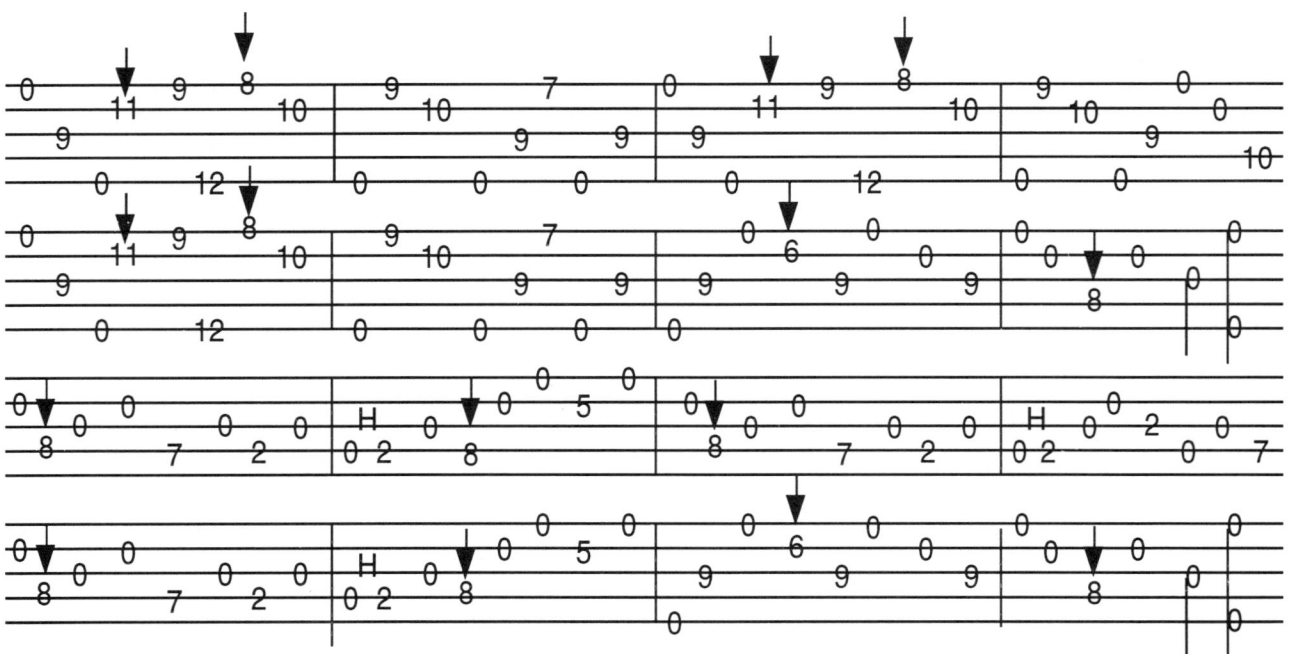

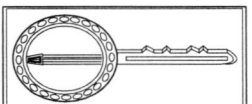

The Key To Five String Banjo

The Dominant Seventh Chord

In the previous chapters, we used five notes from the major scale (1-2-3-5-6), to paint a road map to the neck. This grid paints two different chord types - major and minor - and will be more and more useful as you slowly imprint the pattern into your fretboard consciousness.

You might be asking yourself, "Since we've used five notes from a total of seven in the major scale, aren't there two notes left? What about the other two notes? Don't they count?" Yes! Of course they do! And, as a charter member of the "Musical Note Conservation League," I believe that every note in music counts. We mustn't waste any notes! In fact, I vow to crusade until every note in music is cherished and finds a home in a progression somewhere.

In A class by Itself

The dominant or seventh chord is very special. It usually completes the end of a chord progression. Notice how the remaining two notes from the G major scale (the ones we didn't use in the pentatonic scale) match two of the notes in a D7 chord. The remaining two major scale notes, the 4th and the 7th, are very unique and define the "dominant sound." This is because of the distance or interval between them (6 frets). What makes these two notes so distinctive is that we can find and outline every D7 chord. In other words, F# and C define a D7 chord and the other notes which add variety to it can be located adjacently.

G major scale:

G - A - B - (C) - D - E - (F#) - G
         4   7

D7 chord:

D7 = D - (F#) - A - (C)
     1   3   5   7

The dominant chord is actually the pivot point of all chord progressions. In fact, this "resolving" progression is so important that it is called the "Dominant Progression."

The Dominant Progression is a very practical progression therefore it must be learned thoroughly. Find out how to start using it in the Practical Theory Appendix p. 49.

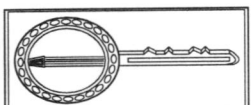

The Key To Five String Banjo

The dominant seventh chord or "seventh chord" (V7 chord) is a harmonically unique chord. To outline all D7 chords, here are two neck forms. The one on the left shows all the "C" and "F#" notes which are solely responsible for the D7 dominant sound. You must "pair" the "C" and "F#" notes to get the basic sound. It only takes one pair to make a chord.

The neck diagram on the right shows these same notes with all the other D chord tones (D and A notes) filled in. If we look at the entire banjo neck and find all "C" and "F#" notes and then relate them to the major chord forms we already know, a total picture is revealed.

Adding notes to the "C/F#" pairs generates D7 chord forms. What is even more interesting is that if you take any pair of "C/F#" and proceed six frets up, the pairs reverse "F#/C" on their respective strings. As long as these two notes are present, you can add other notes from the G major scale to form a more recognizable chord form. The most common notes to add are "D", "A", "E" and "B." Adding these notes in various combinations produces extended harmony. That includes the 9th ("E"), 13th ("B") or suspended 4th ("G") extensions. Extensions do not alter the basic sound but expand and enrich it. On the next page a few D7 chord forms are illustrated. In all these chords the "C" and "F#" notes are labeled.

D Dominant Seventh Chord
D - F# - A - C

38

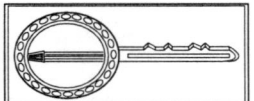

The Key To Five String Banjo

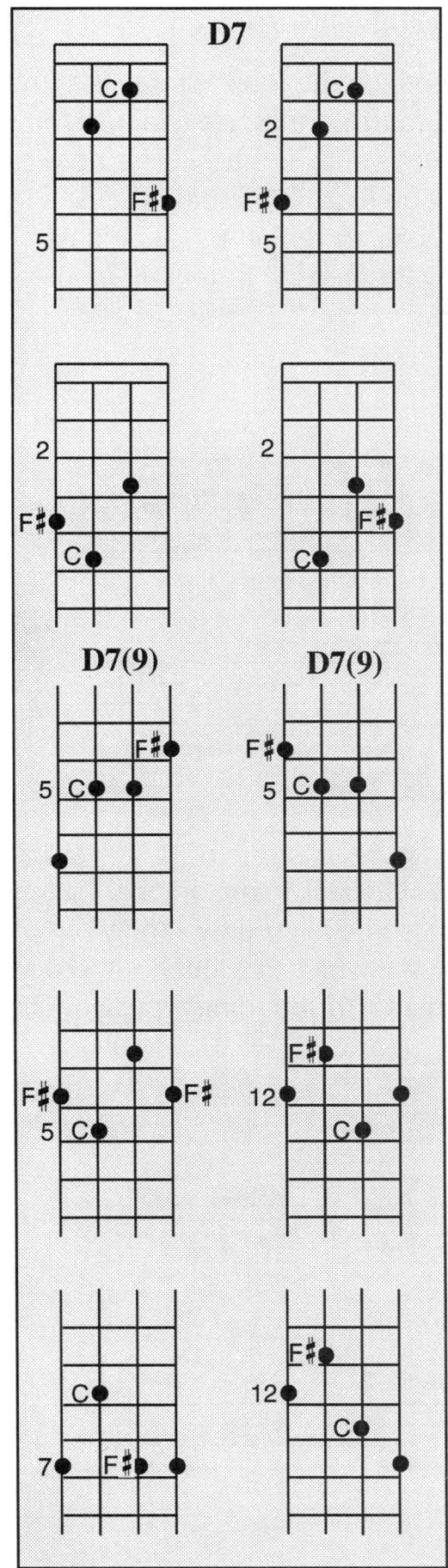

Here are a few three and four note chords extracted from the grid on the previous page. The "C" and "F#" notes are paired and one or two notes are added from a G major scale to make a D7 chord position. G major is the "parent" scale for D7. In other words, a G major scale generates D7 chords and scales.

In each example, play the "C" and "F#" notes *first* and then add the other notes to complete the chord sound. After you have played the two key notes and then the full chord, play the closest G major chord. Practice going back and forth between the D7 chord and the nearest G major chord. This is called the "dominant progression" for the key of G. (D7-G)

Much of music is tension and release. The D7 chord creates tension. The ear seeks resolution to be resolved by the G major chord. It's like the famous "Shave and a Haircut" ending with the "two bits" ending. The "two" is the D7 chord and the "bits" is the G major. Without it, the barber would never get paid!

Playing this progression all over the neck and in as many keys as possible will help you to learn how to resolve. Resolving is basic to all styles from classical and jazz to folk and bluegrass.

Extended harmony is discussed in the Jazzin' It Up Appendix. So why not extend yourself to page 53 and find out what it's all about?

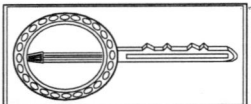

The Key To Five String Banjo

Changing One Note - Again!

The root or first position for D/Bm (D is the lowest note on the fourth string) is at the 12th fret. By changing only one note on the first and fourth strings, we can transform a pentatonic major/minor position into a dominant seventh position. The note to change is the "B" note at the ninth fret. By moving it up to a "C" note (both first and fourth strings) we have the required "C" and "F#" pair to define the dominant D sound. Therefore, changing from the pentatonic Key Positions to dominant involves an alternation of only one note. This one change from "B" to "C" can be made to all five Key Positions resulting in a D7 sound.

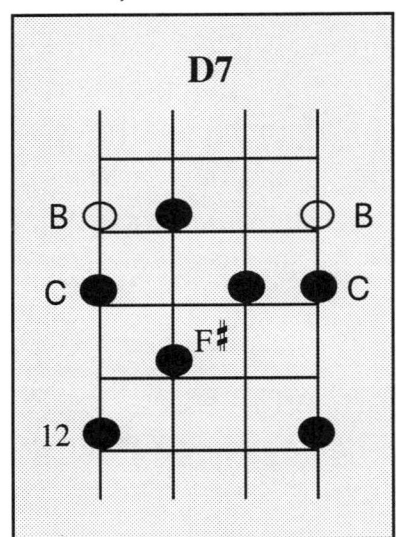
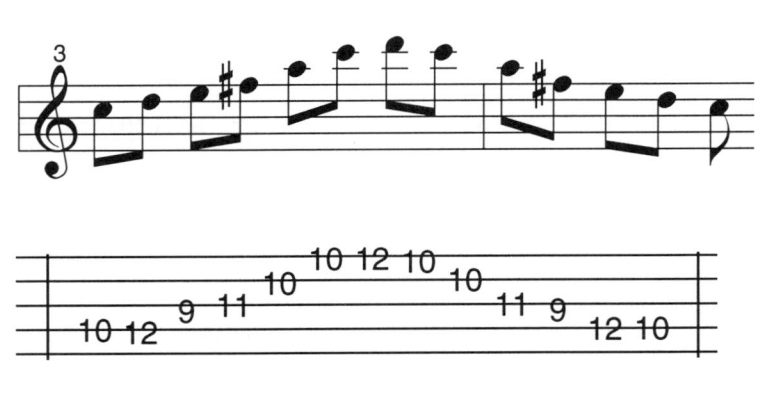

The same process can be used to change G/Em to G7. Go back to the original 1st Key Position at the fifth fret, (p. 14). This G/Em position can be altered by simply raising the "E" note one fret to "F". Below is Key Position #1 which has been altered to include the necessary "B" and "F" notes, resulting in a G7th sounding arpeggio. The "parent" scale now becomes C major.

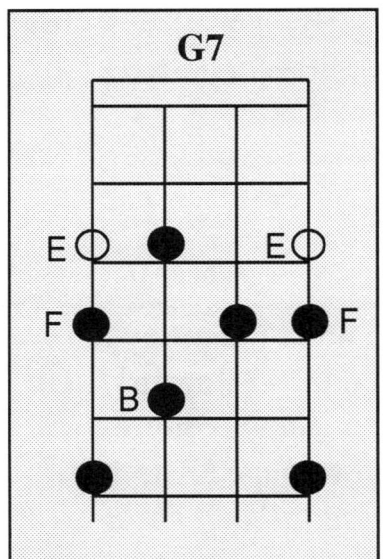

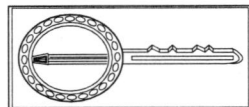

The Key To Five String Banjo

Finally, this alteration will also transform a C/Am position at the 10th fret to C7 ("A" note raised to "B♭").

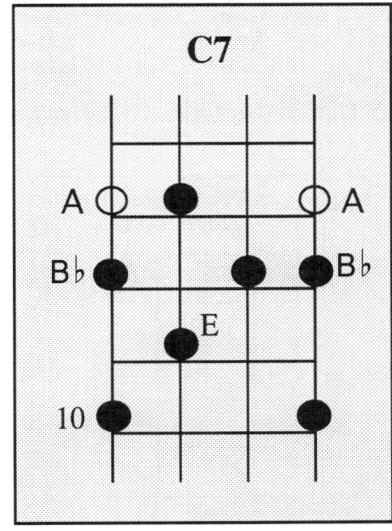

Full Range Fingerings

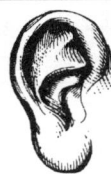

Below are full range neck fingerings for three common dominant seventh chords. Listen to the recording and be able to sing or hum them before playing the tab!

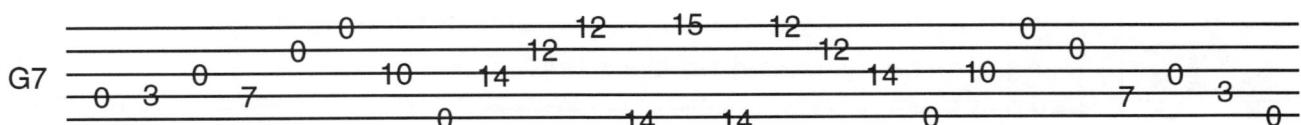

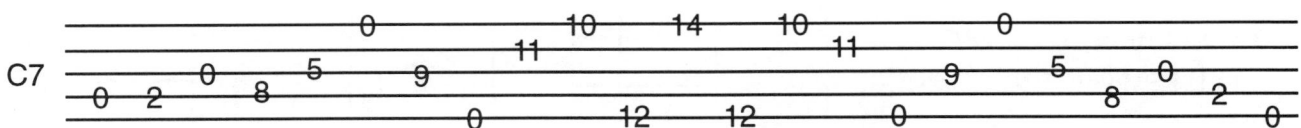

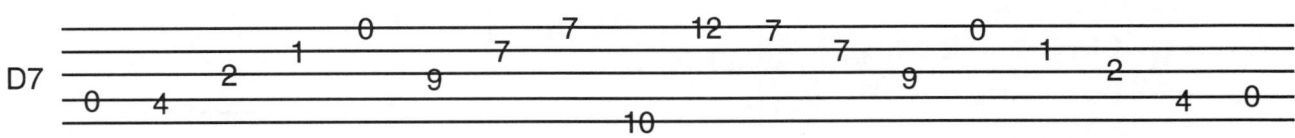

The difference between major and dominant seventh is subtle. Listen for the contrast on the recording first and then try the exercises.

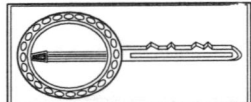

The Key To Five String Banjo

One Fret Blues

With a little creative right hand fingering, you can invent an interesting blues pattern which will fit a number of bluegrass style tunes. I have as my inspiration for this the late, great Don Reno. This progression is a perfect example to demonstrate the harmonic basis of dominant chords. It uses the dominant chord fragments of G7, C7 and D7. You play this blues progression by taking a pair of notes for each chord change and moving the pairs one fret up or down from G7. In the form to the right, G7 is defined by the two notes "B" and "F." The D7 chord is formed around "C" and "F#" which is merely a fret higher!

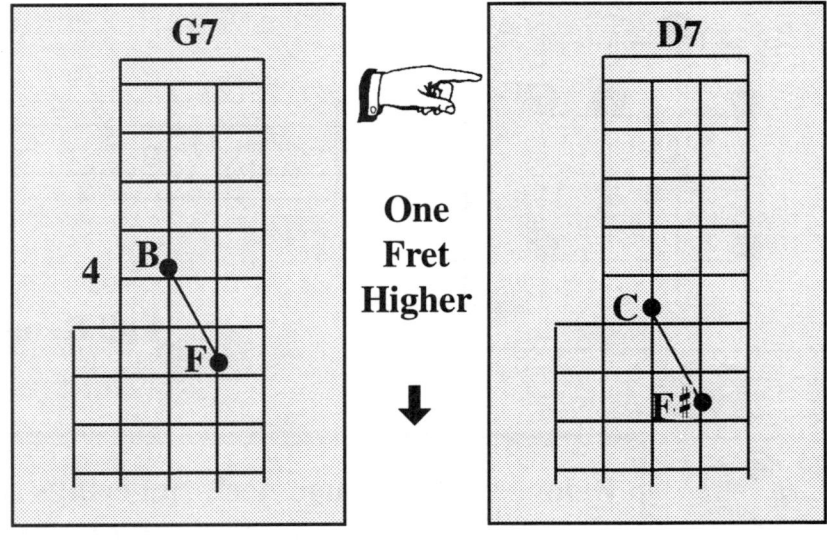

 **Go to the Jazz Appendix and "Riding the Cycle" (p.54) to see the cycle which shows how any two pairs of dominant notes lie adjacent on the cycle and on the neck.**

Simply move both the 3rd and 7th notes of G7th up in pitch one fret to "C" and "F#" and you get a D7 chord fragment. Likewise, the essential C7 notes B♭ and E reside only one fret lower in pitch from the "B" and "F" notes of G7. What could be more simple and direct? On the following page, 12 bar blues progressions in G are tabbed. The illustrations on this page apply to exercise #2. With this two-note principle you can work your way around the cycle. It is a great way to learn all your dominant seventh chords.

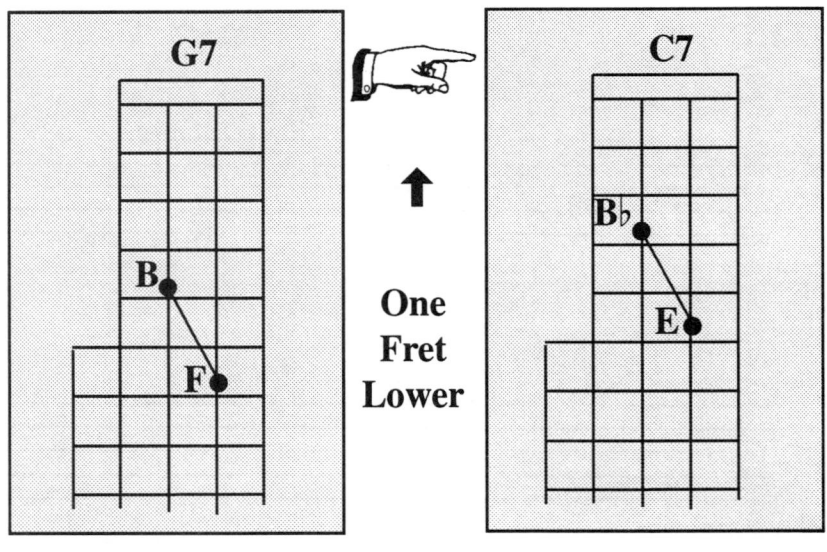

42

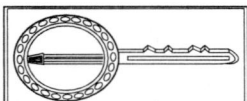

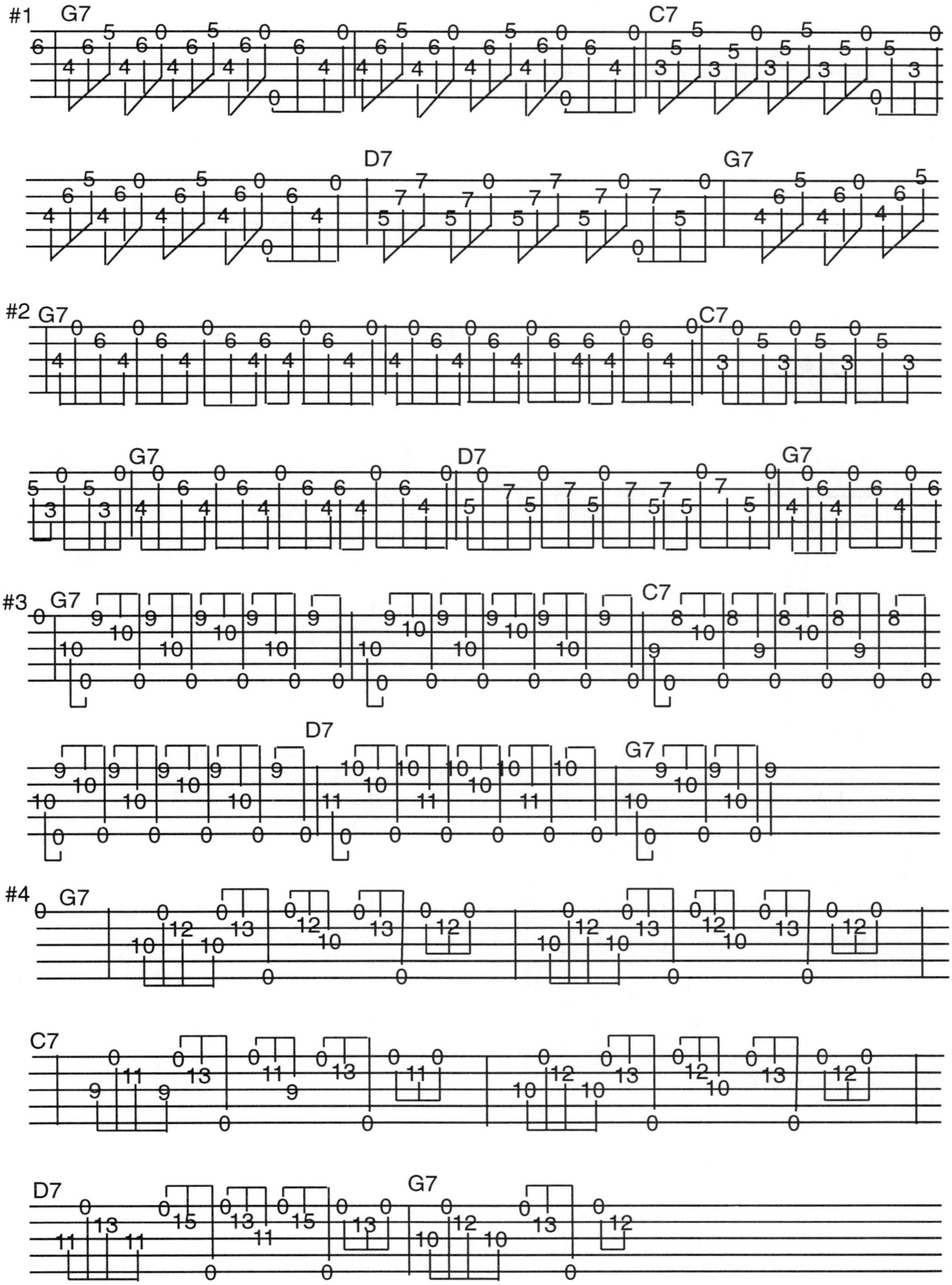

The Key To Five String Banjo

43

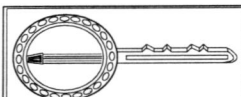

The Key To Five String Banjo

In Conclusion

Finally, here are full neck views of G7 and C7 for a reference. They outline the basic dominant pairs and then illustrate those same note pairs with basic major chords surrounding them. On the following page, some basic G7 chord forms.

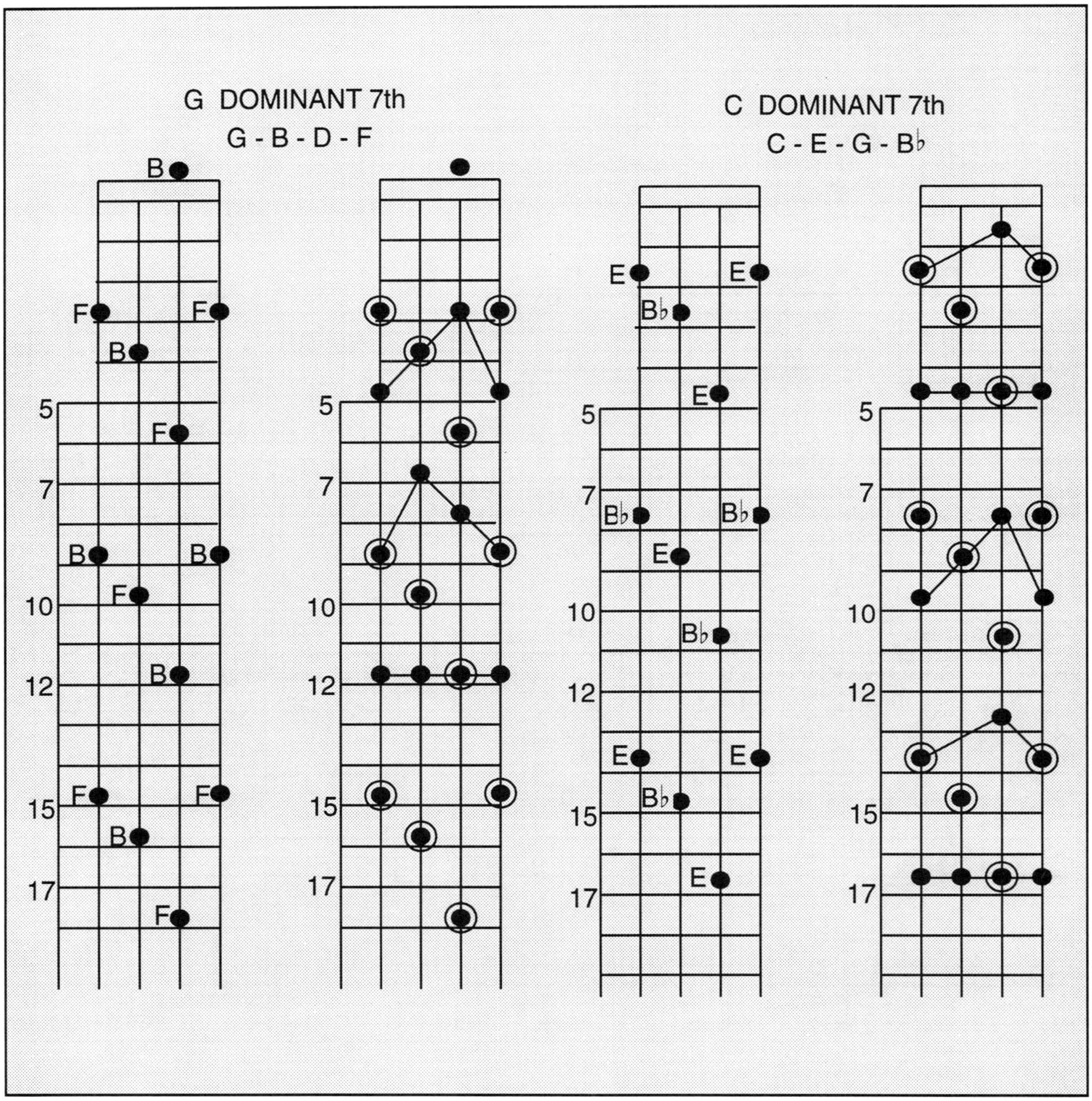

44

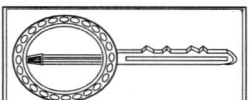

The Key To Five String Banjo

G7 Chords

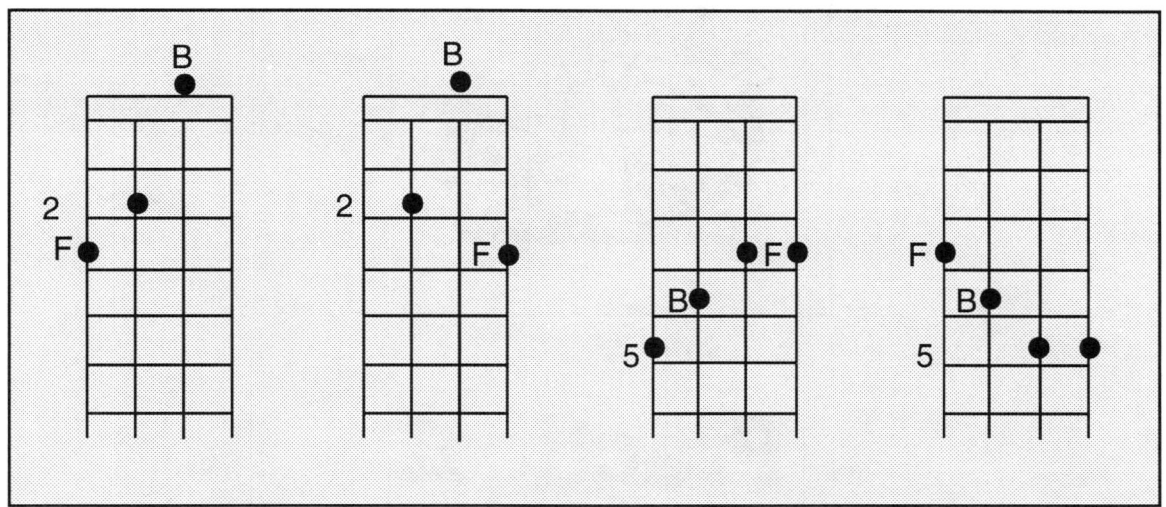

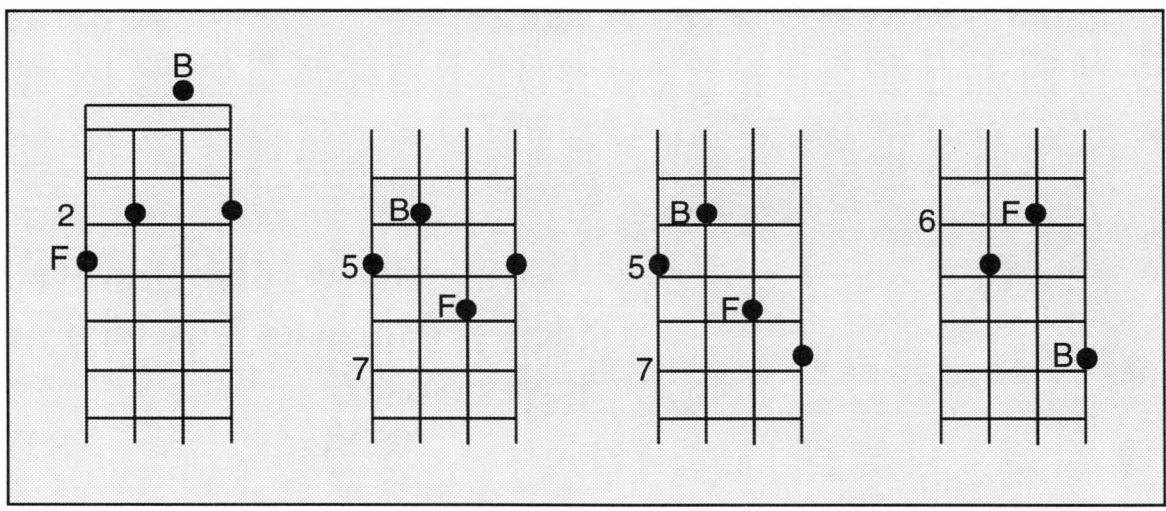

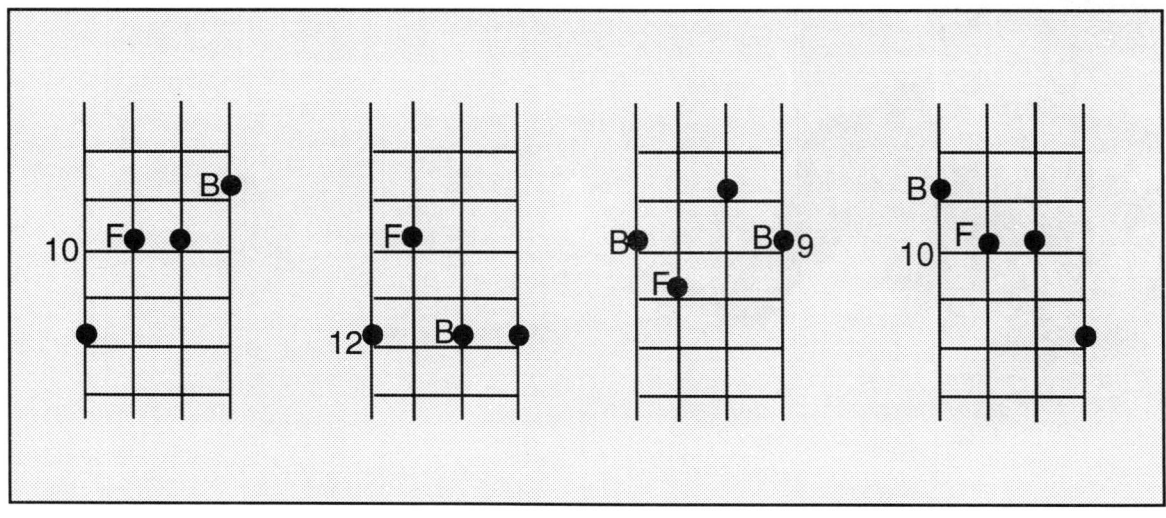

Practical Theory Appendix

"As a rule we disbelieve all facts and theories for which we have no use."

William James, 1897

Major Chord Triads

Chords are derived from scales. The G triad is made up of the notes G-B-D. These notes are pulled from a major scale by starting on the "G" note and skipping every other note to form what is called a root triad. It is called the "root triad" shape because it is three notes. The lowest note on the 4th string also gives the chord its name.

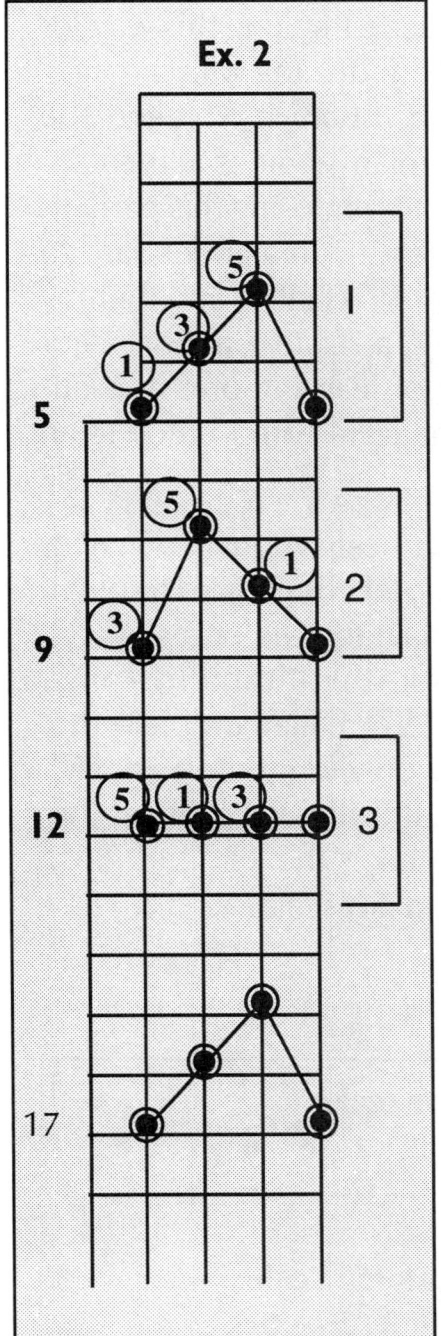

Ex. 2

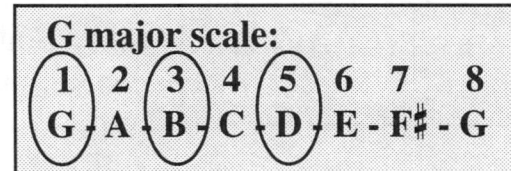

G major scale:
1 2 3 4 5 6 7 8
G - A - B - C - D - E - F# - G

These notes form the familiar slanting triangle position that sits on the 5th fret. The G-B-D is numbered 1-3-5 and represents the 4th, 3rd, and the 2nd strings. The 1st string note, which completes the basic position, is an octave "G." It matches the "G" on the 4th string. An octave means that it is a note twelve frets higher in sound. (Think of the first two notes in "Somewhere Over the Rainbow.")

The second basic formation, which sits atop the ninth fret is called the 1st inversion. The first inversion notes are B-D-G. It is inverted because the lowest note in the stack is a B note on the fourth string. The notes do not retain their original order but they still sound like G triad. Chord tones can be rearranged and still retain their chord sound. The "B' note is on the first string an octave from the "B" on the fourth string. The notes B-D-G are identical to the 3rd, 2nd and 1st strings in the root position inversion above it.

The third major chord formation is a bar at the twelfth position. It is called the second inversion. The notes are D-G-B with the octave "D" on the first string. The diagram to the left shows the Root inversion again at the 17th fret, also an octave above or twelve frets above the 5th fret position. These three chord formations will be essential in forming the grid or road map of the neck.

The Pentatonic Scale

The sound of a pentatonic scale has been described as flowing or like running water.

> E Minor + (7th) = E-G-B + (D)
> G Major + (6th) = G-B-D + (E)

Thinking of a chord form as being dual in regard to the kinds of sound it produces is not new. Guitarists have been thinking this way for years. In this case we are dealing with a major/minor relationship. In theory it is called the "relative minor." The relative minor in this case is Em7 and it is "relative" or related to G major. The reason for choosing this particular relationship to organize is twofold. First, it is much easier and straightforward to learn than a full major scale with seven notes. It will be easier to visualize and thereby organize the notes on the fingerboard. Secondly, by using a relative minor/major system, you are getting two chord qualities for the price of learning one. For our purposes here, a "G major" chord plus an "E" note is identical in composition to an "Em chord" plus a "D" note:

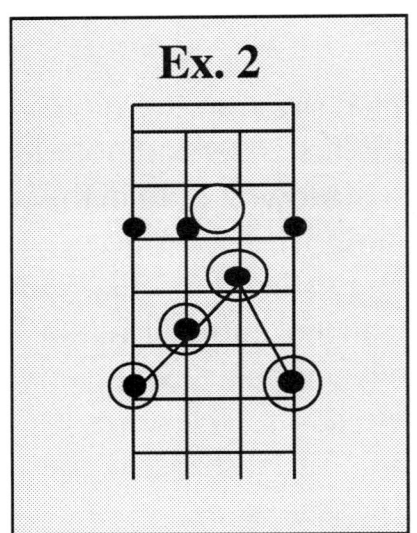
Ex. 2

They could rightly be called musical synonyms. When you play these four notes, the order with regard to pitch is of no consequence. In the diagram, the notes of a G chord are circled. The "E" notes are the 4th and 1st strings at the 2nd fret in the diagram. To make complete the pentatonic scale (we now have only four notes) an "A" note is added. In the diagram, it is the 3rd string at the 2nd fret. The pentatonic scale takes the 1st, 2nd, 3rd, 5th and 6th notes from the G major scale.

This is the first position of a total of five. Each position links to the other and can be used to navigate your way around the neck. These positions "fill in the gaps" between the major chords and will provide you a way to organize the neck.

> **G Major scale:**
> 1 2 3 4 5 6 7 8
> G - A - B - C - D - E - F♯ - G
>
> **G Pentatonic Scale:**
> 1   2   3 5   6
> G - (A) - B - D - (E)

The Dominant Progression

The Dominant progression is very simple. It involves just two chords, the Dominant Seventh chord and a major or minor chord. Below is the dominant progression for the key of G:

G Major scale:	G Dominant Progression:
1 2 3 4 5 6 7 8 (G) A - B - C -(D7)- E - F# - G	V - I D7 - G

In this case, the Dominant Progression is a V chord (D7, the fifth position in the major scale of the key) resolving to the first position, or I chord. What does this mean in terms of sound? All music is a kind of tension and release. When a chord progression wanders away from the "key" or I chord, tension is produced until the progression winds its way back to it again. When it does, the tension is released. The tension is then said to be resolved. The I chord is like a big bag of potatoes. It just sits there. It goes nowhere. Chord movement ceases.

A perfect example of tension and release are the solos on the fiddle tune Orange Blossom Special. The song is in the key of A (I or key chord). The beginning of the song has an extended progression of E7th (the V chord). Each soloist takes as much time on this E7th chord as is necessary to say what they want musically. All the time this is happening, the audience is listening to the soloist ride this E7 train and tension is building up for a musical resolve. When the chord progresses to A (I chord), the tension built up is relieved and the audience usually goes wild. In an unconscious way, the audience is glad to have the tension finally released. This is the power of the dominant progression. Next time you hear a "shave and a haircut" remember that the "two bits" is the D7-G resolution. You wouldn't dare not pay for your haircut, now would you? A lot of unrelieved tension there!

To the right are the twelve Dominant progressions. If you learn them, you will be on your way toward learning to resolve in every key.

V-I
A7-D
B7-E
C7-F
D7-G
E7-A
F7-Bb
G7-C
Ab7-Db
Bb7-Eb
Db7-Gb
Eb7-Ab
Gb7-B

Where Are The Notes On This Thing?

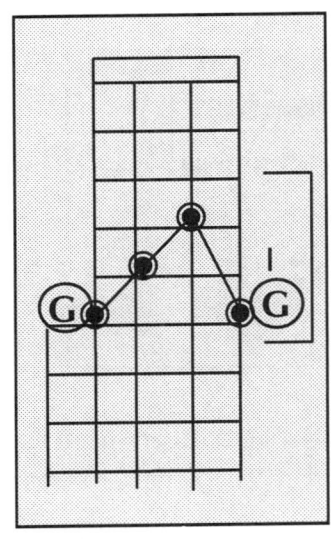

When you play a basic G chord, at least one of the notes in that chord is G. In fact, in the root position, two notes are "G" - the fourth and the first string. So when you play any chord in this position, anywhere on the neck, the name of the chord and the names of the first and fourth strings are identical. In the first inversion on the ninth fret, the name of the chord is the same as the second string. In the bar at the twelfth fret, the chord name and the third string are the same.

Alphabet letters are assigned to notes on the fretboard. This alphabet system is totally arbitrary. Since alphabet letters only represent 7 of the 12 tones, sharps and flats are used to make up the remaining spaces in the 12-tone system.

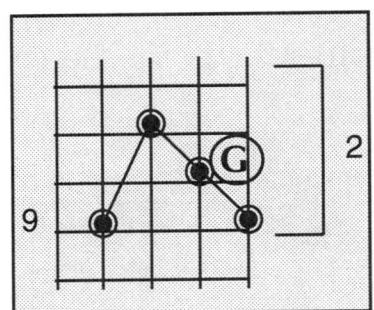

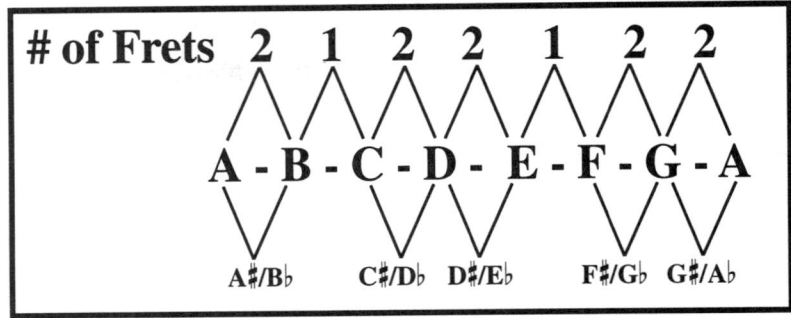

There is one fret (or chord form) between each alphabet letter, except for "B & C" and "E & F which are adjacent". With this exception, all other adjacent alphabet letters have "accidentals" or a sharp or flat between them. To sharp a note means to raise the frequency of its pitch a half-step or one fret. To flat a note means to lower its pitch a half-step. An "A♯" and a "B♭" are the same note depending upon the direction you are coming from. So is "C♯" and "D♭", etc.

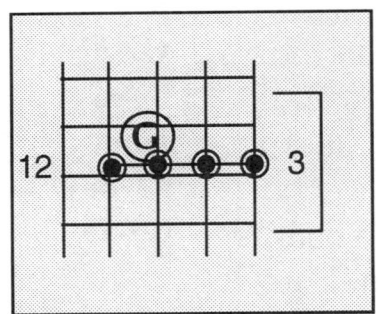

What, then, does this mean? It means that if you know where a G chord is, you can find any note or chord because notes and chords follow the same step pattern up and down the neck. For instance, if you start with open strings, (a bar "G" at the nut) you can find and name all the third string notes and bar chords all the way down the neck. The same goes for the root inversion (1st and 4th strings) and the 1st inversion (notes on the 2nd string).

Jazzin' It Up

Jazzin' It Up

What is Improvisation?

The art of musical improvisation is probably as old as time itself. Before the advent of written musical notation, the interpreting of music first heard in the mind's ear was as natural as speaking. It may be that improvisation is a kind of aural vision for those prophets who were more ear oriented - the ancient musicians of history. Even in the classical tradition, it is said that Mozart and Bach improvised freely. No artist exists in a vacuum. Every artist is a product of the style of the day. Every great improviser absorbs and pays homage to the style and traditions of their time.

The topic of musical improvisation is fraught with mystery and misunderstanding. It is *not* an act of pure spontaneity. Playing spontaneously without knowledge of an instrument, even in the barest sense, would be gibberish. There is indeed an intense process of conditioning and preparation involved with the adapting of one's neurology to the physical problems of a musical instrument. The hours of thought and practice are hidden from the listener. One mistakenly views a live improvisational performance as springing "out of nowhere." Improvisation is a conditioned spontaneity which allows a stream of musical consciousness to pour forth.

What kinds of conditioning are involved?

- ✔ **Use of fragments and patterns from scales and arpeggios**
- ✔ **Invention suggested by a particular melody**
- ✔ **Melodies from other songs**
- ✔ **Patterns and fragments from other players**
- ✔ **Patterns the improvisor is currently studying**

Improvisation involves prehearing the next musical event to be played. Patterns which are known to work in certain musical situations are used. Other notes are comfortable finger habit patterns comprising an improvisers so-called "bag." When a musical idea is heard, the improviser must know exactly where those notes are on the instrument - a kind of instant musical dictation. This also presupposes that there are things heard in the mind's ear worth playing. The melody must be in the ear and in the hand. Patterns and fragments are essential to this end.

Jazzin' It Up

Extended Harmony

Harmony begins with two notes sounded simultaneously. This is called a simple harmony. The span or distance between two notes is called an interval.

Triads, or three note chords, are derived from major and minor scales by selecting every other note and playing them simultaneously. By selecting every other note in the illustrated G seventh scale, you have a basic seventh chord and the beginning of extended harmony.

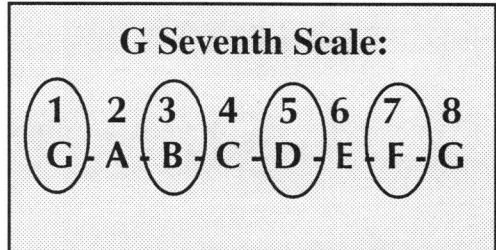

Extending harmony beyond the eighth note or "octave" you form ninth, eleventh and thirteenth chords. On banjo, you usually have only four strings available for chording.

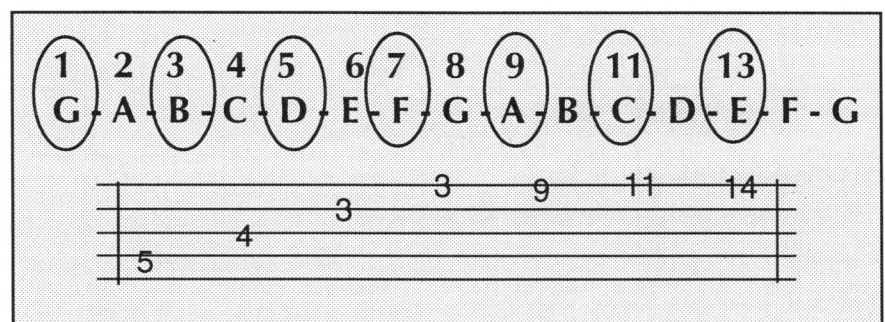

It is not necessary to play every note in an extended chord in order to impart the chord quality. Some notes may be omitted. This does not, however, change the overall chord sound.

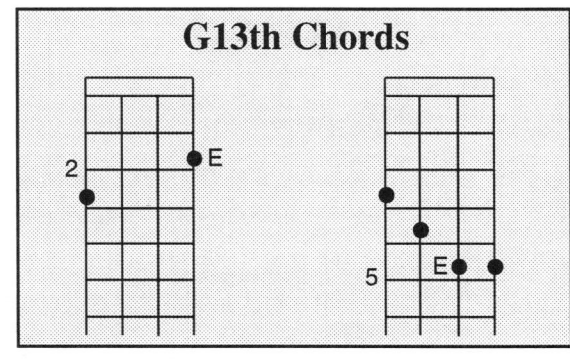

The voicing (note order) does not have to be consecutive as in these diagrams. The ninth and thirteenth formations shown are some of the more useful chord configurations.

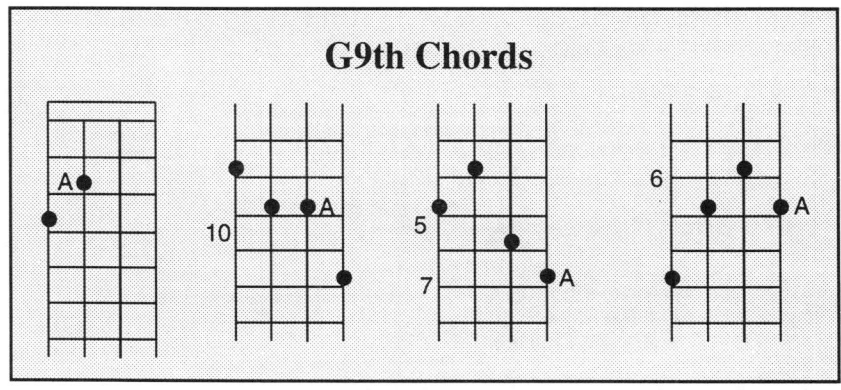

Jazzin' It Up

Riding the Cycle

So what's with this Cycle thing? Why would you want to know about it? So many times, music theory is an enigma. It becomes friendly when its purpose in learning is discovered. It's like we know the sun shines, but only have theories as to why because we can't get close enough to it. But you don't need to know theory of how the sun shines to get a suntan. Music theory was never meant to be an esoteric exercise in speculation and unless it has a practical use, it's a pretty dry read! The cycle is an explanation of how alphabet letters and 12 tones interact to produces keys or tonal centers. Basically, it asks one simple question: If you have a major scale, and are allowed to change only one note in that major scale, what note can you change to get a different major scale and what scale would you get? When understood in these terms, it becomes simple to organize scale practice. Why? If you're learning a specific major scale, changing only one note to access a new major scale makes it easier to learn that new major scale. There are two ways to go. You may sharp a note to get a different major scale, or you may flat one note. On the cycle, C is at the top. A "C" major scale contains alphabet letters with no sharps or flats. Adding sharps around the cycle to the left produces sharp keys and adding flats around the cycle produces flat keys. If you wish to sharp a note in C to get a different major scale, the note to sharp is "F", the fourth note. Sharp the fourth note and start the new scale on the fifth or "G" note and viola! You have a G major scale:

C Major scale:

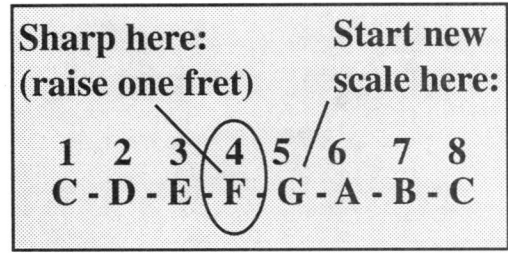

G Major scale:

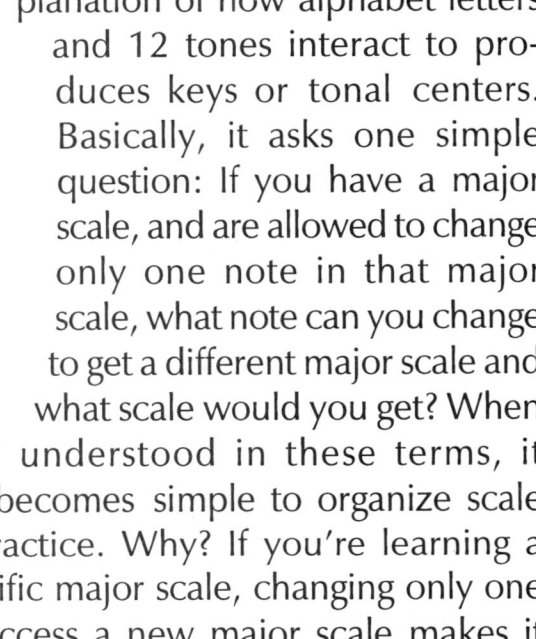

 **Jazzin' It Up**

Riding The Cycle

Now, if you take that G major scale and go to the fourth note "C" and sharp it while keeping the "F#", you create a D major scale or the second scale with two sharps from C in the cycle:

G Major scale:

D Major scale:

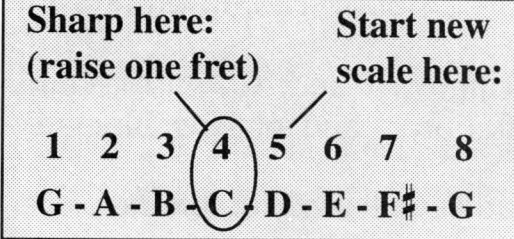
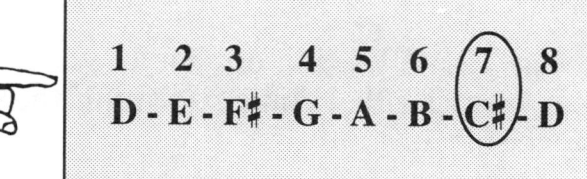

This is the smart way to practice major scales. Adjacent scales in the cycle differ from each other by only one note. Build your way through the cycle, rather than practicing scales "hit or miss." Keep adding sharps in this manner, retaining all the sharps as you go until you arrive at the "F#" at the bottom of the cycle. It is the key with six sharps.

On the other side of the cycle, what note do I flat in a C scale to create another major scale? The answer is the "B" or seventh note of C major scale. Begin the note order on the "F" (fourth note). The result is an F major scale. This starts the cycle in the other direction, retaining all the flats as you go until you get to Gb. It is the key with six flats.

C Major scale:

F Major scale:

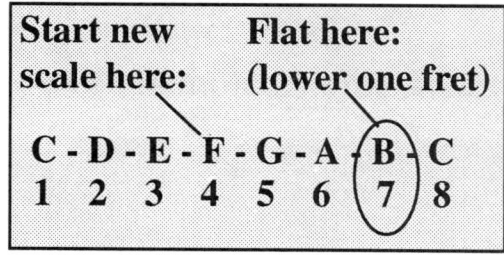
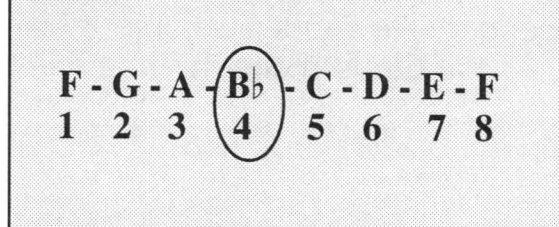

Notice that the cycle is organized in fifths when adding sharps (from C, count five notes C-D-E-F-G) and in fourths (C-D-E-F) when adding flats. The cycle is ear-training as well as an approach to organizing melodic materials. You can practice fragments, phrases, and licks as well as scales and arpeggios utilizing this logic. Most of the structure underlying Western music is based on this concept. Once you learn to utilize and hear it, you will understand and anticipate many common chord changes.

PAT CLOUD

Pat Cloud was born in Los Angeles in 1950 and discovered the five-string banjo by chance at age fourteen when his mother purchased a used swap-meet banjo as a wall decoration. By age sixteen, he was playing professionally and toured with the USO Bob Hope Oriental Command tours of 1967 and 1970 and in the early 1970s, appearances on television include the Tonight Show, Merv Griffin, and PBS. He has been a Los Angeles studio musician for 25 years.

In 1972, he began jazz studies with former Nat King Cole guitarist, Horace Hatchett and then with William Thaisher (co-author of the Joe Pass guitar books), and started to adapt a fluid jazz vocabulary to five-string banjo utilizing melodic technique pioneered by such banjoists as Carrol Best, Bobby Thompson and Bill Keith.

In 1974, he, joined briefly with mandolinist Jimmy Gaudreau and country music great Keith Whitley forming the "New Tradition" band playing Bluegrass throughout the southeast.

Between 1976 and 1980, he continued jazz studies with jazz vibraphone player Dave Pike and continued in the Los Angeles studio circuit along with associations with the Walt Disney Corporation and the UCLA jazz workshop.

In 1983, he recorded the album "Higher Power" with Barry Solomon and Bob Applebaum on the Flying Fish label and was nominated that same year in the best "new instrument" category by Downbeat Magazine.

He is included in the 1988 Oak publication, Masters of the Five-String Banjo, in which Tony Trishka says:

"He is the first five-string player to achieve a wide-reaching command of the jazz vocabulary, and as such inhabit a rarefied world which he now shares with a select few. To hear him play is amazing, but to watch him elicit those streams of "boppish" notes from a predominantly bluegrass instrument is other-worldly."

In 1989, he was awarded "Banjo Player of the Year" by the California Country Music Association.

In 1992, he participated in the Tennessee Banjo Institute with other banjo notables including John Hartford, Douglas Dillard, Carl Jackson, Grandpa Jones, Bill Keith, Taj Mahal, Mike Seeger, Ralph Stanley, Tony Trishka, Doc Watson, and legendary New Orleans banjoist Danny Barker.

Pat Cloud makes his home in the Eastern Sierras in central California.